OpenSpace Beta
Silke Hermann I Niels Pflaeging

BetaCodex Publishing

Silke Hermann | Niels Pflaeging

OpenSpace Beta

A handbook for organizational transformation in just 90 days

First edition

BetaCodex Publishing, Wiesbaden

The BetaCodex Publishing series:

Volume 1 – Niels Pflaeging: Organize for Complexity.
        How to get life back into work
        to build the high-performance organization, 2014
Volume 2 – Niels Pflaeging I Silke Hermann: Complexitools.
        How to (re)vitalize work
        and make organizations fit for a complex world, 2018
Volume 3 – Silke Hermann I Niels Pflaeging: OpenSpace Beta.
        A handbook for organizational transformation in just 90 days, 2018

Cover & book design: Niels Pflaeging
Illustrations & timeline design: Ingeborg Scheer, dasign.de
Additional illustrations (cover, p. 25, p. 27): Pia Steinmann, pia-steinmann.de
Back cover photo: Janik Happel
Copy editors: Deborah Hartmann Preuss, Francois Lavallée, Valentin Yonchev, Jeremy Brown and Matt Moersch

Distributed in Europe, UK, the US/Canada, Australia and worldwide
by BetaCodex Publishing
ISBN 978-0-9915376-6-2

BetaCodex Publishing books are available at special discounts when purchased in bulk for events and conferences as well as for fund-raising or educational use. Special editions or book excerpts can also be created to specification.
For details, send an e-mail to contact@betacodexpublishing.com

Version 1.1. - Argyris

Visit our websites:
www.OpenSpaceBeta.com I www.betacodexpublishing.com I
www.silkehermann.com I www.nielspflaeging.com I www.betacodex.org

OpenSpace Beta timeline

Sponsor

Facilitator

Formally Autho-rized Managers

OpenSpace roles

Participants

Conveners

Master of ceremonies

60 days

Build-up (Set stage!)

Preparing executives

Socializing the invitation (45 days)

Theme crafting

Coaching role begins

Draft & send invitation

OpenSpace meeting 1

Beginning (Prepare!)

Day 1: Opt-in meeting

☑ yes
☐ no

Day 2: Prep day

Proceedings OS 1

Practi

Practicing Beta team patter

BetaCodex constraints

OpenSpace Beta© and the OpenSpace Beta© timeline by Silke Hermann & Niels Pflaeging. Illustrations: Ingeborg Sch

uencers
utationers

Teams

e Beta roles

OpenSpace roles

aches

Stakeholders

days

OpenSpace
meeting 2

Ending (Check!)

30 days

pping - learning (Do!)

Quiet period (Level up!)

creation
gthening

Proprietors
of power in action

Day 1 & 2:
Opt-in meeting

Coaching
role ends

e-boxed
pping

Chapter
debrief

Deliberate
storytelling

arning
leration

Theme
& invitation

Proceedings
OS 2

Recurring
OpenSpace

"Without passion, nobody cares.
Without responsibility, nothing gets done."

Harrison Owen

Contents

Contents (continued)

Acknowledgment:
Daniel Mezick & OpenSpace Agility

Only a couple of months have passed since our first encounter with Daniel Mezick, in May 2018. It is hard to come across a fresh, sophisticated concept that is as well fleshed-out, and as well-explained as Daniel´s *OpenSpace Agility*. When we met Daniel, and got talking about inviting, non-coercive approaches to change, we immediately sensed the potential of his core approach for what we call Beta transformation.

OpenSpace Agility has been a booster to our creativity: It kick-started the development of OpenSpace Beta. Thanks to the creators of OpenSpace Agility and the handbook that accompanies it, we were able to conceive OpenSpace Beta and this handbook in just a few months, from idea to market.

We borrowed a lot from the wonderful book by Daniel and his co-authors; we modified a lot of details, took out a few things, and added roughly 30% of Beta-related stuff. Through remixing & tweaking, we transformed Daniel´s original concept to serving transformation of entire organizations, regardless of size.

We are thankful to Daniel for his radically open-source approach to innovation, which we share and cherish! Daniel's generosity, and his willingness to share experience and conceptual insight have been unusual. We think that his spirit of radical sharing is exemplary for a new era of collaboration that we all long for. It is this spirit of all-in collaboration that we urgently need, if we want to shape the future of work, together.

What´s so cool about this:
While the overall approach of OpenSpace Beta is new (it blew our minds quite a few times while we figured it out for ourselves!), all the concepts within the approach are research-based and practically tested. Everything we present in this book has been tested and done, by ourselves throughout our 15 years of working on Beta organizations, by Daniel and by the other OpenSpace Agility creators and practitioners.

Our special thanks go to all the authors of The OpenSpace Agility Handbook, a rich and innovative resource that has been the foundation of the book you are holding in your hands. *The OpenSpace Agility Handbook* proved to be such a great resource that we were able to use it as a model for several of the sections of this book, and tweak other parts, in order to make them fit for Beta-style, full-fledge, organizational transformation.
Thank you for letting us use the OpenSpace Agility Handbook and web text as a baseline resource: Mark Sheffield, Deborah Pontes, Harold Shinsato and Louise Kold-Taylor.

For more about their work, visit *www.OpenSpaceAgility.com*

Foreword - by Daniel Mezick

Silke and Niels are doing something remarkable with this book: they are spreading an idea whose time has come. And that idea is a very simple one: the idea that it's the passionate and responsible people that create real change. It's the idea that willing people actually make everything happen. The people who say "yes" to an invitation.

The idea of the invitational Open Space meeting and using it in organizations appeared in the 1980s. According to the tale often told, Harrison Owen "discovered it" while enjoying two martinis and reflecting on life. A little later on, he wrote his first book, entitled: *Spirit: Transformation and Development in Organizations*. Harrison always did his best to keep Open Space truly open and free. Good news travels fast, and thousands of Open Space events took place, worldwide, over the next 30 or so years.

Then I showed up. At the time, I was an "Agile coach" looking for a better way. By 2010, I was sure that "Open Space" was that better way. And I started experimenting. I discovered that you can get very strong results if you arrange two Open Space events about 45 to 90 days apart, with some space in between, for the whole group to figure things out.

And from that idea, "Prime/OS" was born: a method for creating an environment, in enterprises of all sizes, where rapid, authentic and lasting change can be achieved. I formalized the idea and started teaching it to people. I published all of it under a free, "open source" license to encourage people to innovate and improve on the basic idea.

Then Niels and Silke showed up. They immediately recognized the power of recurring and iterative Open Space events to manifest change in organizations. They asked for my permission and support with making use of Prime/OS and the OpenSpace Agility Handbook, and I gladly agreed. The result is this remarkable little book, and the free-to-the-world, "open source" licensing of their remarkable "OpenSpace Beta" definition, derived from Prime/OS.

Daniel Mezick is an author, executive and Agile coach, and keynote speaker.

He is the formulator of *OpenSpace Agility* and *Prime/OS*. He is co-author of *Inviting Leadership*, and the author of *The Culture Game*, a book describing 16 patterns of group behavior that help make any team smarter. The *Culture Game* book is based on five years of experience, coaching 119 Agile teams across 25 different organizations. Daniel´s client list includes CapitalOne, Intuit, the Hartford, Cigna, Siemens Healthcare, Harvard University, and many smaller enterprises. Daniel is based in Guilford, Connecticut.

Web: www.DanielMezick.com,
Email: dan@newtechusa.net

The beauty of what Silke and Niels have done is profound.
First, they have created the conditions where the BetaCodex mindset will always stick, no matter what. That's because the Open Space "wrapper" encourages experimentation, innovation, and self-organization. Second, they are publishing the core ideas of OpenSpace Beta under a free "open source" license. This license allows you to innovate and create something new. They are literally inviting you to study their work, derive from their work, improve upon it, and make an all-new creation if you so choose.

We live in a time when we need more freedom, not less. More innovation, not less. More collaboration, not less. We need more progress, not less. More openness, not less.

So go ahead. Study this book.
Start with OpenSpace Beta. Try things. Take a shot.
Because you never know what might happen if you try.

Daniel Mezick,
August 2018

How to use this book

Welcome to the OpenSpace Beta handbook! The purpose of this handbook is to serve as a handy reference and as a pocket guide for those who are adopting the Beta organizational model or otherwise using OpenSpace Beta to bring strength and vitality to their Beta adoption efforts.

This book is for anyone who is interested in creating more rapid and lasting Beta transformations. This includes company executives, directors, managers, team managers and the consultants and coaches who serve them.

Throughout most of this book, pages with white background indicate content on roles and activities. Pages with light green background indicate more abstract, conceptual content.
You may prepare for using this book in several ways:

- Have a basic understanding of the laws of the BetaCodex and how Beta can help your organization. Part 1 of this book will provide you with *Conceptual background to OpenSpace Beta*: This is especially worth reading if you are new to Beta. Part 6 of this book, entitled *Practicing - flipping - learning (Do!)*, discusses the BetaCodex laws, or principles. The *www.betacodex.org* website provides many resources about this, too.
- Have a basic understanding of the OpenSpace (OS) meeting format. OpenSpace Beta© and the Prime/OS™ framework behind OpenSpace Beta are inspired by the work of Harrison Owen, specifically by his book *Spirit: Transformation and Development in Organizations*. It is a great work, full of keen insights and actionable ideas. It should be of strong interest to anyone who is serious about organizational systems, organizational dynamics and culture. The *Spirit* book is available online as a free PDF download at *www.openspaceworld.com/spirit.pdf*.
  Part 2 of this book includes a brief user's guide by Harrison Owen.
- A bibliography of important books related to OpenSpace Beta appears at the end of this book. The *Terminology* section in Part 1 will help you with key vocabulary. Visit *www.betacodex.org* for information about Beta certification and additional learning resources on Beta.

Origins of OpenSpace Beta - and what you can do with it

OpenSpace Beta® derives from Prime/OS™ - an open source culture technology which was developed by Daniel Mezick and published under the CC-BY-SA-4.0 license. More about Prime/OS™ can be found here: www.Prime-OS.com and www.OpenSpaceAgility.com/about

OpenSpace Beta® and Prime/OS are freely available, open-source, culture technologies: You are free to derive from OpenSpace Beta™ and create innovative new works yourself and share your innovations with others and even commercialize them.

OpenSpace Beta™, the open-source OpenSpace Beta timeline, events, rules, roles, meetings, consulting techniques and related documents are published under the *Creative Commons Attribution Share-Alike* license. This license is an open source license: Under this license, you are strongly encouraged to innovate by freely developing applications based upon OpenSpace Beta.

About the license *Attribution ShareAlike – "CC-BY-SA"*: This license lets you remix, tweak and build upon OpenSpace Beta, even for commercial reasons. In so doing, you agree to:

- credit the original authors, Silke Hermann and Niels Pflaeging and
- provide our specified link to the source material, as listed below and
- license your derivative creations to others under the identical terms.

Specifically, you must provide and prominently display the following link with any and all derived works and included as part of all related graphics you develop: *"This work is derived from OpenSpace Beta®, an open source culture technology published under the CC-BY-SA-4.0 license and found here: www.OpenSpaceBeta.com"*

{ OpenSpace Beta and the underlying Prime/OS are open source social technologies. Remix & tweak them. Build upon them! Then share again! }

Bye-bye coercion, hello engagement! The Why of OpenSpace Beta

Mandating reduces engagement. Invitation and opt-in participation increase it. Engagement is essential for rapid and lasting Beta transformation. OpenSpace Beta, consequently, is based on invitation, instead of mandating specific Beta practices.

Prescribing practices makes no allowance for what people want, what they think, or what they feel. Prescription reduces engagement: The intelligent and creative people who do the work "check out" and disengage.

People doing the work in organizations today are well-educated. They were hired for a reason - usually because they are intelligent, qualified and capable. Such people resist imposition of change (not the change itself!), but they often will not articulate their views. Instead, they may either ignore directives ('internal sabotage') or walk away completely. Corrective notions of "improving communications" and "achieving better buy-in" completely miss the point: What is needed is to invite the relevant workforce to co-create the organization's development together, as a collaborative iterative effort, with everyone's perspective valued.

How can we invite a whole large organization to co-create change at scale? It can only work through an approach based on consistent self-organization, within a framed structure of iterations and intentional intervention on all levels of the system, which fully engages the relevant workforce constructively throughout all of the work. This is achieved by applying the principles of OpenSpace Technology at the beginning and the end of the timed iterations, combined with the principles of the BetaCodex.

The OpenSpace Beta pattern calls the Sponsor to:
- Explain the case for transformation, or for moving in the Beta direction. Explain the challenges the business is facing in terms of competition, pricing pressure, organizational effectiveness, etc.
- Make it clear the organization *will embrace Beta principles.* Explain that specific practices have *not* been determined.

- Invite everyone involved into the process of writing the Beta transformation story. Communicate clearly that the managers do not have all the answers and that they are looking for the very best ideas to make the move to Beta genuine, authentic, rapid and lasting.
- Make it plain that the organization will work with a wide array of Beta practices. The results of each intervention on the system (or "Flip") will be inspected to determine whether to continue the specific practice. If a practice does not meet the needs of the team or the organization, it can be changed or discarded. The teams are even free to "roll their own" practices. The only constraint is that the practices must align with the BetaCodex.

By adopting Beta principles this way, the people doing the work have a strong sense of control, belonging and purpose. They engage.

You do not get to self-organization through method that relies on imposition. If you want to create a truly great and truly high-performing organization, there is no way around Beta, or disciplined self-organization. To get to Beta, in turn, you need an approach to transformation that itself is coherent with BetaCodex principles (page 109), too. Such an approach must be consistently self-organized and engaging.

{ OpenSpace Beta in itself is an invitation. It is based on invitations, personal responsibility and self-organization. }

Part 1

Conceptual background to OpenSpace Beta

(There is nothing as practical!)

Self-organization and assumptions on human nature

In his book *The Human Side of Enterprise,* published back in 1960, Douglas McGregor presented a key message: That we hold two images of human nature in our heads and in our hearts - Theory X and Theory Y. And that one of these images, Theory X, is a fraud. McGregor stressed, on every page of that book: Theory X people (which supposedly have to be motivated extrinsically) do not exist in the real world. They have never existed, do not exist and will never exist: They are merely a figment of our imagination. Theory X, by consequence, although common as an image of human nature we hold dear, is no more than an ugly prejudice about other people at work.

Even 60 years after McGregor's book, however, most people claim and firmly believe, that "Theory Xers" exist around them. Inevitably, they act accordingly, making the world a worse place than it could be. We stubbornly adhere to a myth that McGregor tried to dispel back in 1960; we apply method that would only work with Xers. We are stuck in a world of Theory X delusion. Most of us are guilty of perpetuating the Theory X prejudice.

The good news: 100% of actual people are Theory Y people. The world is full of them, and they long to be treated as the self-motivated people they are. They strive on engagement, which is the fuel of rapid and lasting Beta transformation. Mandating of Beta practices, on the other hand, reduces the potential for genuine engagement, and it has the potential to ruin your Beta transformation. It is for "Xers". Without an opt-in feature to the game, the game of transformation is not "well-formed" - which makes it less fun to play. Invitation is a far better approach, as it aligns with the BetaCodex laws, or principles. Invitation increases engagement by offering options, as well as a sense of control and a feeling of belonging, which are sources of basic human happiness. Opting in or out of an Invitation increases the sense of control. Accepting an Invitation increases the sense of inclusion.

{ OpenSpace Beta is a "good game", partly because of its opt-in nature. Invitation can engage the independent thinkers in your organization. They are the ones who help create traction for Beta. }

Org Physics:
The 3 structures of organizations

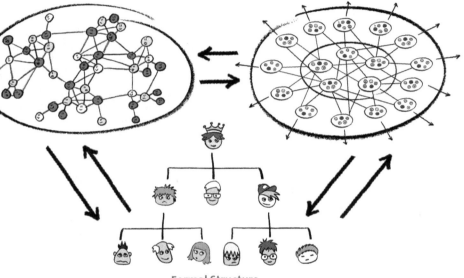

Informal Structure
Domain of human relationships
Social/relationship power = Influence
Power holders: Influencers

Value Creation Structure
Domain of work & performance
Power of those with mastery = Reputation
Power holders: Reputationers

Formal Structure
Domain of compliance
Power of position = Hierarchy
Power holders: (Formally Authorized) Managers

Every organization has three structures. There is no decision to make about having all three of these structures, or not: None of the three structures is optional, or nice to have. They are part of what we call organizational physics - universal laws that apply to every organization, large or small, old or new, for profit or social, everywhere in the world.

The three structures of organizations are carriers of three kinds of power, and three kinds of leaderships that are present in every organization.
- Formal Structure is the domain of compliance. Power held in this structure is referred to as hierarchy. This is the structure that is most

Org Physics:
The 3 structures of organizations (continued)

commonly referred to as "our structure", in most organizations. Sadly, it is often wrongly assumed that work or value creation can be organized, or improved, through formal structure. Even though this structure is useful only for organizing compliance, or "being within the law". We call leadership in this structure "Compliance Leadership."

- **Informal Structure is the domain of the social within the organization.** Power held in this structure is commonly referred to as influence. It is social power held by those with social relationships inside the organization. Informal Structure is neither good, nor bad. It is.
  We call leadership in this structure "Social Leadership."

- **Value Creation Structure is the domain of work, performance, competitiveness, and innovation.** Power held in this structure is referred to as reputation. It is the power of those with mastery. Organizational performance can only emerge from this structure with its outside-in/inside-out relationships, and team constellations within Periphery and Center. It is here where "flow" happens. It is here where value creation can be strengthened, and waste fought against.
  We call leadership in this Structure "Value Creation Leadership."

The three structures of organizations are interdependent. Every member of an organization is present in all structures. In Formal Structure, every person typically holds one position. In Informal Structure, that person operates a personal web of social relationships. In Value Creation Structure, that very same person holds several roles, within one or more team or cell constellations. Effectiveness of interventions within an organization's system can be increased by examining in advance the structures in which these interventions will interfere, and by examining what reactions within the three structures are likely to occur. It is also useful to ask, for every flip, or intervention in the system, who from one or more structures is needed to increase the likelihood of a certain desired outcome.

{ Interventions in the system, or flipping, may impact one or more of the three structures - or none. }

Decentralization & team autonomy

In complexity, organizations must be federative, or decentralized. When outside markets reign, it is the organization´s periphery that necessarily earns the money, learns from the market and adapts quickly and intelligently to external market forces. The center - isolated from the market by the periphery - loses its knowledge advantage. In these conditions, it can rarely give useful orders and the steering collapses. The linkage between periphery and center must be designed accordingly, so that it becomes possible to assimilate and process market dynamics. For that, the periphery must steer the center through internal pull, or demand-supply relationships. The periphery must be sovereign of the organization´s resources.

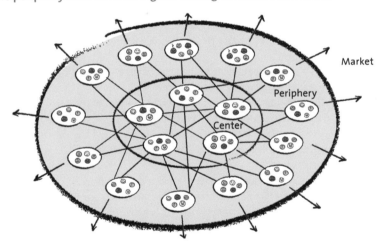

In "decentralized mode", the need for having a middle management disappears entirely. Here, self-organization and leadership from the outside-in become possible.

{ In the principle of decentralization, the devolution of autonomy and decision-making power to the periphery goes on and on. Decentralization never ends. }

Learning, change and the neutral zone

Profound change is a transitional state of being for an individual. William Bridges called this transitional state the Neutral Zone. It cannot be skipped.

Even though there might be a heightened sense of awareness, and lots of energy, it is a no-man's land of transition, confusion, stress, and vagueness. It lacks definition. No longer where you were, and not yet where you will end up, the Neutral Zone has the potential to drive people crazy.

Because learning in Beta is constant, Beta transformations generate a steady stream of stressful "in-between", or Neutral Zone experience. That may generate a lot of stress in the organization. Learning is change, and change is stressful because it triggers Neutral Zone experiences.

The Neutral Zone is a stressful state of being that occurs in transitions. Beta transformation requires everyone to adopt new ways of thinking and acting - pretty much at the same time. This intertwined individual experiences of the Neutral Zone can cause considerable worry and anxiety. As a solution, OpenSpace Beta uses a well-understood cultural device called the Rite of Passage, to channel actions in the Neutral Zone and reduce stress.

Adopting Beta always means lots and lots of new learning. Learning itself can be perceived as de-stabilizing and stressful, because it means going through transition. All genuine learning in adults creates instability and stress, until that learning is integrated.

Mental models

We know the world through our models. Mature adults hold millions of models of reality, and genuine new learning challenges the validity of at least some of these models. This invalidation of previous assumptions produces an unstable state (often referred to as "cognitive dissonance") until the new understanding is integrated.

The adoption of a Beta organizational model definitely creates cognitive dissonance, and the need for executives, directors, managers, and Team members to step into the Neutral Zone. The introduction of Beta is usually a trigger for most Participants. This "triggered" behavior may be based on all kinds of emotions, including excitement and fear - and is a natural reaction to entering the unstable state of the Neutral Zone.

Before Beta, roles and methods of interaction were well understood. New roles and new ways of interacting require a new mindset. The process of learning can be stressful. When faced with an uncomfortable transition, the natural and safe thing to do is turn around and go back. People in organization routinely do or try exactly this. They may backslide on Beta and (try to) return to where they came from. This "going back" in the short term reduces worry, fear and anxiety, some of the core emotions evoked by the Neutral Zone.

Rites of passage

Rites of passage are cultural rituals or games. A rite of passage is a ritual whose structure defines a beginning, a middle and an end of a transitional experience. Rites of passage have been enacted for thousands of years to deal with stressful transitions of human experience. OpenSpace Beta employs a rite of passage that begins and ends with an OpenSpace meeting event. This, plus the other mechanics of the 90 days, brings structure to the chaos associated with integrating new learning.

Tribal societies, as well as modern societies throughout the world and accords different periods have reached the exact same conclusion: The Neutral Zone must be framed and handled carefully. The best way to handle it is with a rite of passage. The purpose of such rites of passage is to ease, not to eliminate, the transition from one state of being to another. In the modern day, we routinely introduce change into organizations, while bliss-

Learning, change and the neutral zone (continued)

fully ignoring the essential human dynamics of the Neutral Zone. This is a serious error - one that we are keen to avoid in OpenSpace Beta.

Designing a rite of passage is an exercise in experience design. Rites of passage serve as containers that reduce the highly destabilizing feelings of the Neutral Zone. This matters, because stress can lead to all sorts of problems, including deep anxiety, fear, even panic.

Rites of passage usually include at least one rather scary experience. For example: A member of a tribe going through a rite of passage from boyhood to manhood might have to kill a dangerous animal, or prevail in the wilderness by himself for a while. You might be wondering if such a notion of a passage-rite is a good idea for an organization: Do we really want to put people through potentially dangerous experiences? But rites of passage are not an end: They are a means, or cultural responses, to the reality that highly stressful transitions exist and must be dealt with intelligently, in the context of a society or an organization. The rite of passage serves to contain the already-scary experience of transition. They are established by social groups in response to the need to deal with highly stressful Neutral Zones. Transitions are part of our reality - the rite of passage is not an option, but a cultural mechanism for dealing with the transition. The stressful and necessary transition - for example, the transition from childhood to adulthood, is present before the rite of passage was instituted.

In other words, a rite of passage itself does not produce stress. Instead, a rite of passage structures the Neutral Zone that arises through key transitions in the life of individuals, or throughout the existence of a group, or organization. The rite of passage structures the unstructured and thus provides some comfort in difficult times.
The primary task of a Beta transformation is to produce organizational transformation for high performance. This is a profound transition that - in theory and in practice - never ends, because it is focused of continuous, never-ending learning and improvement. It is perpetual Beta.

Framing these highly complex transformations and the arising dynamics within them is challenging. Which is why OpenSpace Beta must acknowledge these dynamics, and employ rites of passage, to help people, Teams and the organization to make the transition to a new state. The rite of passage must be designed with clear objectives, clear boundaries (or principles), rich feedback and Opt-in participation.

Robustness in the Neutral Zone

A hypothesis of OpenSpace Beta is that introducing Beta into a typical organization induces Neutral Zone experiences at the individual, the Team, and the organizational levels. If this Neutral Zone is handled with a rite of passage, there is potential for a rapid and lasting Beta adoption.

A core idea behind OpenSpace Beta is that recognizing and addressing the Neutral Zone smartly reduces the worry, anxiety, and fear associated with Beta adoption. The rite of passage creates a structured experience for Participants with a beginning, a middle and an end.

OpenSpace Beta is a repeatable technique for getting a rapid and lasting Beta adoption. It works with what you are currently doing and can be added at any time. It incorporates OpenSpace, rites of passage, Game Mechanics, Deliberate Storytelling and more, so your Beta transformation can take root.

Spirit of community

Beta transformations thrive on strong feelings of "spirit of community". When the spirit of community is "up", the space is open. When the spirit of community is "down", the space is closed. Example: If you love going to work, the overall spirit at work is probably "up". If you cannot wait until Friday, the overall spirit in that workplace is probably "down".

Learning, change
and the neutral zone (continued)

With respect to Beta transformation, this spirit of community is essential. It comes from clearly understood and uniformly applied principles (not: rules). It comes from a sense that everyone should be engaged. It comes from a sense that "we are all going through this together".

During Beta transformations, everyone is being triggered. What is my role? What are the principles, or the "rules of the game"? When does this end? What does this mean for my status in the group? Executives and managers are triggered. Team members are triggered. In the Neutral Zone of new principles, new roles and unfamiliar ways of working, is it any wonder that Beta transformations have been hard to achieve?

Cultural anthropology holds that people going through a rite of passage do in fact have the same status *during* the passage, while Participants have widely varied statuses *going in*. While all are coming from diverse, known places and going to an unknown place, all of them make the difficult and even dangerous passage together. And after it is over, all have changed from what they were to what they now are. All of the individuals go through the rite of passage experience with its beginning, middle and end. They experience it together, regardless of level of status or authorization. Everyone is learning.

{ Rites of passage such as OpenSpace Beta are intentionally designed cultural experiences, or cultural experience designs, designed to invoke feelings of community. }

Work as a game

Work and organizations can be viewed as games: If the core requirements for self-fulfillment are not present, then people will likely disengage and check out. If the core requirements are there, people are likely to experience fun, satisfaction and potentially a deeply engaged sense of well-being. OpenSpace Beta delivers organizational models, or systems, apt for human self-fulfilment through the intentional design and implementation of good Game Mechanics.

Work is "broken" when it is not fun to play. Deliver self-effectuation, or self-fulfilment at work by injecting good Game Mechanics into the structure of work and meetings. That in short, is a way of describing Beta.

The core requirements for good Game Mechanics, or self-organization:
- A sense of control.
- A sense of progress.
- A sense of belonging and membership.
- A sense of wider purpose and meaning.

When viewed in this way, it is possible to more fully design the interactions, meetings, and work itself so that participating is optimized toward a satisfying, fun, and naturally productive experience.
OpenSpace Beta employs Game Mechanics to the change experience itself, to make Beta transformation itself as enjoyable and fun as possible.

Games have four basic properties. When values for each of the properties are "well-formed", then the game is enjoyable, fun, and satisfying. When the four properties are not "well-formed", the game is not fun, and people either opt-out, or, if this is not possible, they disengage ("check out") almost automatically.

This disengagement is often tagged "resistance to change", in conventional change management. It is not a resistance to the change itself, though, but a logical consequence of bad Game Mechanics.

Work as a game (continued)

The four basic properties of a good game are:
- A clear goal
- A clear set of principles that are uniformly applied
- A clear way to get feedback and to track progress
- Opt-in participation

Well-executed Beta patterns and practices are usually (but not always) well-formed games. Well-formed games associate with satisfaction, happiness, and even joyfulness; poorly defined games associate with disengagement, low levels of learning and a distinct lack of enjoyment.

OpenSpace Beta makes organizational change easier by making it a good game. The key gaming component is the Invitation, which is used instead of a mandate. Participants are invited to practice Beta patterns, instead of being forced to use them without being part of the decision-making.

Work and organizations are games, and in Beta, this spirit is devolved to them. Beta transformation itself is a game, too. To make Beta transformation fun, we must tune up the four properties above. In OpenSpace Beta the constant focus on Game Mechanics (as opposed to coercion) is essential.

{ OpenSpace Beta frames the Beta experience as series of interrelated games. It supports and strongly encourages practicing and genuine playfulness. What is really going on is play, and play is fun. }

Terminology

OpenSpace Beta is built on a couple of core ideas from sociology, psychology, cultural anthropology and organizational sciences. These concepts cannot be described in detail in this handbook, and they have been elaborated well in the works from the Recommended Readings section.
These are some of the terms that appear in this book.

Alpha. The opposite of *Beta*. Also commonly referred to as command-and-control, or pyramid organization. Alpha is based on the assumption that organizations can and must be steered from the top down, dividing between thinkers at the top and doers at the bottom. Governed by management the social technology, Alpha worked well enough in the industrial age, but ceased to work in the higher complexity of the knowledge age. The overwhelming majority of organizations is still in Alpha mode. Just as the Beta mindset, Alpha can be articulated through an indivisible set of 12 laws or principles.

Authority Projection: The almost automatic characterization of the OpenSpace Beta coaches and consultant (acting as Master of Ceremonies) as an authority figure, often leading to various impediments to progress within the client organization.

Beginning OpenSpace. An OpenSpace event that begins a Chapter of Learning. The beginning OpenSpace is also known as OS 1.

Beta, or BetaCodex. Beta is the organizational mindset that is fit for complex markets and fit for human beings. The Beta mindset is articulated through the BetaCodex - an indivisible set of 12 laws or principles.

Chapter, or Chapter of Learning. A unit of organizational learning with a clear beginning, middle and end. In OpenSpace Beta, a Chapter of Learning happens between two OpenSpace meetings (OS 1 and OS 2) and lasts 90 days.

Coach(es). An external person to assist in learning Beta principles, methods and practices. A strictly temporary role in OpenSpace Beta.

Terminology (continued)

Complexitools. Organizational methods that are inseparable from human beings: Complexitools are as alive and as complex as the problems we try to solve with them. An example of a Complexitool is OpenSpace. Others are Relative Targets or Organizational Hygiene.

Deliberate Storytelling: The act of filling a social space with meaning with intent to reduce anxieties and worries in the organization.

Economic buyer: The person in a client organization signing the cheque for effectively engaging outside support. While OpenSpace Beta does not require conventional external consultants, the roles of Master of Ceremonies and Coach(es) will usually be filled by external advisors. Usually, the Economic Buyer will also fill the Sponsor role within OpenSpace Beta.

Ending OpenSpace. An OpenSpace event that completes and ends a Chapter of Learning. The ending OpenSpace is also known as OS 2.

Facilitator, or OpenSpace Facilitator: In OpenSpace and other meeting formats, a role occupied by a person who works to make the process easier for members to participate in and enjoy. A person authorized by the Sponsor to assist in executing an OpenSpace meeting. OpenSpace Facilitators help create an atmosphere of openness and safety and "hold the space" open throughout the entire OpenSpace meeting.

Flipping, or Flips. Flipping means deliberately intervening on an organization's system, flicking it from Alpha mode to Beta mode. Through flips, we "work the system of work, intentionally" - eliminating, strengthening or introducing system elements. Flips can often be quickly enacted.

Game Mechanics: The specific features of a game that define how effective the game is in creating engagement. Well-formed games have well-formed game mechanics, especially the following features: clear goal(s), clear rules, a clear way to track progress and opt-in participation.

Group Dynamics: A community of practice focused on the study of leadership, authority and unconscious processes in groups.

Influencer. A person holding influence, or one that is liked by others and possesses relationa/social power. Influence emerges within Informal Structure.

Invitation. In OpenSpace Beta, the opportunity offered by Formally Authorized Managers, to act or engage in an activity. Typically, this means attending an organizational event, or participating in a process. Genuine invitations do not have sanctions or any other implied or expressed (negative) consequences for not accepting.

Leadership, or Leaderships. Happens in the space between people. The term "leader", in this sense, is an oxymoron. Should only exist in plural ("Leaderships") because it emerges within each of the three structures of organizations - Formal, Informal and Value Creation Structures. See *Org Physics*

Leveling Up. From the realm of gaming: Progressing or graduating to a new level. Here: a new level of competence.

Mandate: In a process of organizational change, a command or other communication that creates compulsory participation without regard for what the participant wants, thinks or feels. Sometimes conflated with, but very different from, *Invitation*.

Master of Ceremonies. In a rite of passage, an essential role. The Master of Ceremonies understands the phases of changing from one state to another, reassures the Sponsor and participants of where they are in the transformation and ensures that they continue to follow the agreed-upon rules of the Chapter. In OpenSpace Beta, this role will be occupied by an OpenSpace Beta Practitioner - typically, an organizational consultant and trusted advisor.

Neutral Zone: An unstable state of transition between two states. A person experiences the Neutral Zone when they are engaged to be married, quit smoking, changing jobs or moving their residence from one place to another. An organization is said to be in Neutral Zone when it is moving from one way of thinking and working to another, for example during the initial stages of adopting new methodologies, organizing structures or processes. Uncertainty and ambiguity about the new way may lead to confusion and stress. For more, see *Bridges, William: Managing Transition*

Open Source: A type of license that promotes attribution, innovation, community and collaborative effort, while respecting the work of creators and contributors. OpenSpace Beta© and *Prime/OS*™ are published as open source culture technologies.

OpenSpace. A meeting framework that encourages self-organization. The OpenSpace format is designed to generate very high levels of engagement. It does so by getting all the people with a sense of passion and responsibility in one place, at one time, to address matters of importance to all Participants. OpenSpace Beta uses OpenSpace to maximize *Invitation* and engagement.

Opt-in Participation: A truly voluntary choice to participate in response to an invitation. In a game, a feature of "good-game" mechanics. All good games have clear goals, clear rules, a way to track progress and opt-in participation. See also *Invitation, Mandate*

Org Physics. Organizations have three structures (Formal, Informal & Value Creation Structure), from which three kinds of power (Hierarchy, Influence & Reputation) arise and three kinds of leaderships (Compliance, Social & Value Creation leadership). The three structures are interdependent.

Rite of Passage. In cultural anthropology and in societies generally, a ritual in which the social status of the participants changes. In OpenSpace Beta, a ritual for handling the stress of changing to a new way of thinking and working. Rites of passage help people enter understand and embrace the new way. OpenSpace meetings and periods of practicing with Beta practices serve as rites of passage. The OpenSpace Beta methodology facilitates the design and construction of a rite of passage for teams and organizations. See also *Neutral Zone, Master of Ceremonies*

Patterns. According to systems theory, organizations do not consist of people, but only of people's communication. This communication is not chaotic or unstructured. It happens within patterns that are emergent, and ultimately cannot be controlled by an organization's members. In OpenSpace Beta, intentional and intense irritation of existing patterns through practicing, learning and flipping is possible.

Proceedings. Documentation of the sessions contained within an OpenSpace meeting. Proceedings include participant names, words, diagrams and pictures that describe what was discussed in each session.

Quiet period: In OpenSpace Beta, a period of 30 days following a 90-day passage-rite period. The rite of passage in OpenSpace Beta starts and ends with an OpenSpace event of at least 1 day. During the Quiet Period, the OpenSpace Beta advisor(s) (*Master of Ceremonies, Coaches*) do not communicate with the organization and external advisory work halts.

Reputationer. A person holding reputation relevant for value creation, or one that is recognized by others for possessing mastery. Reputational power emerges within an organization's Value Creation Structure.

Signal Event: In OpenSpace Beta, an action by Formally Authorized Managers that signals a shift in the organizational model, in the direction of more openness, more enterprise-wide dialogue, more innovation across the organization.

Sponsor. A person in the organization with enough authority to convene and invite people to an OpenSpace event that lasts at least one full day.

Part 2

OpenSpace Technology:
Roles & key ideas

(With an introduction by H. Owen)

About OpenSpace Technology

OpenSpace Technology - sometimes referred to as OST - is a design for an all-hands meeting. For over 30 years, groups ranging in size from 50 to 2.000 have opened space and solved complex problems in more than 124 countries around the world.

OpenSpace events are most successful when the organization has:
- A puzzling, complex problem of very high importance that is of interest to the group.
- A passion for resolution, high diversity and the possibility of conflict.
- A response time of "yesterday".
- An organizational model that is not fit for the future.

This meeting format is perfect for kicking off new Beta adoptions and for re-starting, re-making and rebooting struggling Beta transformations.

OpenSpace Technology is based on invitation, respect, opt-in participation and above all, self-organization. Honoring these principles leads to high levels of engagement as the participants join together in writing the story of their Beta transformation. It is their story.

Self-organization scales. OpenSpace Technology leverages self-organization. Frameworks and prescriptions, by contrast, do not scale. Forcing people to do things does not work well.

OpenSpace Beta begins and ends each passage-rite period of intense Practicing - Flipping -Learning in OpenSpace. These one-day or two-day meetings can consist of 20, 50, or more discussion sessions, depending on the group. Be prepared to be surprised!

{ OpenSpace was conceived as an approach to organizational development. It became popular as a conference technology. With OpenSpace Beta, OpenSpace is coming home. }

A brief user's guide to OpenSpace Technology: Introduction by Harrison Owen

This excerpt of the *Brief User's Guide* by Harrison Owen is reprinted here with permission of the author. Serious readers are encouraged to examine the fuller and more complete *Open Space Users's Guide 3rd Edition*, also from Harrison Owen. It is available in print and ebook editions.

***

The requirements of OpenSpace

Open Space Technology requires very few advance elements. There must be a clear and compelling theme, an interested and committed group, time and a place and a leader. Detailed advance agendas, plans and materials are not only unneeded, they are usually counterproductive. This brief User's Guide has proven effective in getting most new leaders and groups off and running. While there are many additional things that can be learned about operating in Open Space, this will get you started. Some material has been included here which also appears in the book in order to present a relatively complete picture.

The theme. Creation of a powerful theme statement is critical, for it will be the central mechanism for focusing discussion and inspiring participation. The theme statement, however, cannot be a lengthy, dry, recitation of goals and objectives. It must have the capacity to inspire participation by being specific enough to indicate the direction, while possessing sufficient openness to allow for the imagination of the group to take over.

There is no pat formulation for doing this, for what inspires one group will totally turn off another. One way of thinking about the theme statement is as the opening paragraph of a truly exciting story. The reader should have enough detail to know where the tale is headed and what some of the possible adventures are likely to be. But "telling all" in the beginning will make it quite unlikely that the reader will proceed. After all, who would read a story they already know?

The group. The group must be interested and committed. Failing that, Open Space Technology will not work. The key ingredients for deep creative learning are real freedom and real responsibility. Freedom allows for exploration and experimentation, while responsibility insures that both will be pursued with rigor. Interest and commitment are the prerequisites for the responsible use of freedom. There is no way that we know of to force people to be interested and committed. That must be a precondition.

One way of insuring both commitment and interest is to make participation in the Open Space event completely voluntary. The people who come should be there because they want to be there. It is also imperative that all participants know what they are getting into before they arrive. Obviously they can't know the details of discussions that have yet to take place. But they can and should be made aware of the general outlines. Open Space is not for everybody, and involuntary, non-informed participation is not only a contradiction in terms, it can become very destructive.

This raises the obvious question of what to do with those people whom you want to involve, but who, for whatever reason, do not share your desire. There are two possibilities. The first is to schedule two sessions, and trust that the first one will be so rewarding that positive word of mouth testimony will draw in the recalcitrant. The alternative is to respect the wishes of those involved. In the final analysis it remains true that genuine learning only takes place on the basis of interest and commitment, and there is absolutely no way to force any of that.

The size of the group is not absolutely critical. However, there does seem to be a lower limit of about 20. Less than 20 participants, and you tend to lose the necessary diversity which brings genuine interchange. At the upward end of the scale, groups of 400 work very well, and there is no reason to believe that number could not be increased.

Space. The space required is critical, but need not be elaborate or elegant. Comfort is more important. You will need a room large enough to hold the entire group, with space to spare in which the participants may easily move about. Tables or desks are not only unnecessary, but will probably get in the way. Movable chairs, on the other hand, are essential.

The initial setup is a circle with a large, blank wall somewhere in the room. The wall must be free from windows, doors, drapes, and with a surface that permits taping paper with masking tape. The wall should also be long enough so that the total group may stand before it, and never be more than three to four deep. The center of the circle is empty, for after all we are talking about Open Space.

If the room is very large, additional break-out areas may not be required, but they are always helpful. Best of all is the sort of environment in which there is an abundance of common space. If you are going to use a conference center or hotel, find one with plenty of conversation nooks, lobbies, and open grounds, where people may meet and work undisturbed, and without disturbing others.

Time. The time required depends on the specificity of result you require. Even a large group can achieve high levels of interaction combined with a real sense of having explored the issues in a matter of eight hours. However, if you want to go deeper than that, reaching firm conclusions and recommendations (as would be the case for strategic planning or product design), the time required may stretch to two or three days.

More important than the length of time is the integrity of the time. Open Space Technology will not work if it is interrupted. This means that "drop-ins" should be discouraged. Those who come must be there at the beginning, and stay for the duration if at all possible. By the same token, once the process begins, it cannot be interrupted by other events or presentations. These might come before or afterwards, but never in the middle.

***

The basic structure

Although it is true that an Open Space event has no pre-determined agenda, it must have an overall structure or framework. This framework is not intended to tell people what to do and when. Rather, it creates a supportive environment in which the participants can solve those issues for themselves. Minimal elements of this framework include: Opening, Agenda Setting, Open Space, and Conclusion. These elements will suffice for events lasting up to a day. Longer events will require the addition of Morning Announcements, Evening News, and probably a Celebration.

A standard Open Space Design, using all these elements appears below. If the event you anticipate lasts longer than the time indicated, simply replicate the middle day. If shorter, you will find that an Opening, Open Space, and Conclusion will suffice. Generally speaking, the minimum time required is five hours, but that is cutting it rather close.

Opening. We have found that a very informal opening works well, especially if the group involved is an intact work group. An evening meal and a time for catch-up conversation will effectively set the stage. Should the group not have any prior association, the simple device of having all the participants introduce themselves by giving their names and telling a short story from their lives to illustrate who they are will usually do the job. Detailed and involved "ice breaking" exercises do not seem to work very well, and, more to the point, set the wrong tone. After all, we want Open Space.

Agenda setting. This is the time for the group to figure out what it wants to do. The details for this procedure are given below.

Open Space. Is exactly what the words imply, open space and time for the group to do its business. There is literally nothing here at the start.

Announcements. A short period every morning for the group to catch up on what it is doing, where, when, and how. Nothing elaborate, no speeches, just the facts, nothing but the facts.

Evening news. This is usually a time for reflection and occasionally fun. Not to be confused with a formal report-out session, the approach is "What's the story?" - with participants voluntarily providing the tale.

Celebration. If your Open Space event is like all the ones we have seen, particularly multi-day affairs, by the last night it will be time to celebrate, otherwise known as having a party. Even in "serious" undertakings like preparation of the corporate strategic plan, when it is over, it is over, and people will enjoy celebrating that fact. We suggest doing the celebration in the spirit and manner of the rest of the event. All of which means don't plan it in advance. It may be worthwhile to have some taped music if your people are inclined to dance, but other than that you will undoubtedly find that the talent you need is already available in the folks you have. Use it. Skits, songs, humorous reviews of what has happened, will amply fill the evening, and add to the learning experience.

Closing. We try to keep the closing simple and serious. Simple in that there are no formal presentations and speeches. But serious, for this is the time for announcing commitments, next steps, and observations about what the event has meant. The closing event is best conducted in a circle with no "head table." Start anywhere, and go around the circle allowing each participant, who wants to, the opportunity to say what was of significance and what they propose to do. But do make it clear that nobody has to say anything. In very large groups, hearing from everybody is obviously impossible, but two or three folks may be asked to volunteer.

Formal reports. The formal report-out session has apparently become a fixture of conference life. However, we find it to be boring and generally non-productive. There is never enough time for each group to say all they wanted to, and if sufficient time is allocated, the majority of conference participants are uninterested at any given time. As an alternative, we recommend using a simple word processing system, a computer conferencing system, or both.

In a recent conference 200 participants created 65 task force reports (a total of 200 pages) which were available as the participants left the conference. Mechanically, all that is required is a bank of computers (low-powered laptops will do) and a request to each group organizer to enter the results of their deliberations into the system. They can either type it in themselves, or for the "non-typables," a small group of secretaries will do the job. We print out each report as it is entered and hang it on the wall, providing an ongoing, real-time record of the discussions. The obvious advantage here is that participants find out what is happening, as it is happening, rather than waiting until the end when it is too late. Of course, having the proceedings at the end of conference, rather than six months later, is a pleasant and positive surprise.

Meals. You will notice that meals are not listed on the agenda, nor are there any coffee breaks. The reason is quite simple: once the conference starts to operate in small groups, there is usually never a time when something of substance is not going on. And in accord with the Third Principle, it will take place in its own time. All of this creates a small, but not insoluble, problem for such things as meals and coffee-breaks. Our solution has been to have coffee and other refreshments available in the main meeting room, so people partake when they are ready. No need for the whole group to get into lockstep, and stop an important discussion just because it is coffee-break time. Likewise with meals. We suggest buffets, open and available over a several hour period, so people can eat when they want to. There are two exceptions to the flexible meal/coffee-break schedule: an opening dinner if there is one, and dinner on the last night.

The whole point is that the pacing and timing of the conference must be determined by the needs of the group and its learning process, and not by the requirements of the kitchen.

***

Facilitators can read more about how to open and hold the space in the original User's Guide by Harrison Owen, available at *www.openspaceworld.com/users_guide.htm*

Authority and self-organization in OpenSpace

Every social situation has an "authority dimension".
OpenSpace creates a very social situation, and therefore OpenSpace has this "authority dimension".

The dynamics and distribution of authority in OpenSpace are really very simple. There are three basic roles: the Sponsor, the Facilitator and the Participants.

- The Sponsor (aka Host) welcomes the group of Participants and authorizes the event.
- The Sponsor then hands over authority to run the meeting to the Facilitator.
- The Facilitator, in turn, then directly hands that authority over to the Participants: to each individual in the group. The Participants play a very active role in the "management" of the event.

The Facilitator does hold back one small piece of the authorization that comes from the Sponsor. That one piece of authority held by the Facilitator is the authority to "hold the space". To "hold the space" is to "hold the space open" or to "maintain openness."

How this "holding the space" is actually achieved can take many forms, and it varies from Facilitator to Facilitator. It also varies from situation to situation. What we know for sure is that, in an OpenSpace event, at least in theory, Participants are free to enjoy the event as they see fit. Participants engage in the event as they wish, without interference from others who might tell them what they"should" do.

{ OpenSpace events encourage very high levels of self-organization
by creating a set of rich and fertile conditions
where self-organization can emerge spontaneously. }

OpenSpace roles

OpenSpace Technology provides a lightweight template for arranging and holding great gatherings and meetings.

OpenSpace Technology only has four roles.
These roles define boundaries and provide guidance about opening up space for self-organization to occur. There is no coercion in OpenSpace.

- The Sponsor authorizes the event, makes it clear that the organization values the event and its outcomes and grants authority and responsibility to the Facilitator for presiding over the event. Then the sponsor gets out of the way and lets the OpenSpace event unfold.

- The Facilitator receives authority from the Sponsor to execute the event from start to finish. The Facilitator retains authority and responsibility for holding the space and keeping it open for self-organization. All of the remaining authority and responsibility for the success of the event are transferred to the Participants.

- Participants self-organize as they decide to attend sessions, participate in discussions and share the outcomes with the rest of the organization.

- Conveners are Participants who propose and initiate session topics for small-group discussions. Within each session the Convener is responsible for keeping the session open for input from all Participants. Conveners are responsible for collecting Proceedings.

The Sponsor

The OpenSpace Sponsor has the most challenging and essential role in OpenSpace Beta. Without an appropriate Sponsor, your transformation can and will face challenges.

An effective Sponsor must be:
- A Formally Authorized Manager with enough authority to schedule an all-day meeting and to authorize attendance for all those invited.
- Willing to fill the Sponsor role completely by taking up all of the duties and tasks that come with it.
- Passionately ready to process and act on the Proceedings with others immediately after the event.

The Sponsor has important responsibilities before, during and after the OpenSpace event, as follows.

Before
- Invite others to help craft the Theme and discover who feels passionate and responsible about the design and preparation of the OpenSpace event.
- Draft and send the invitation to all members of the organization who will be part of the Beta transformation. By personally sending the invitations, the Sponsor indicates the importance of the event. Delegating this responsibility would indicate the Sponsor has "more important things to do."
- Engage in active "deliberate storytelling" about the OpenSpace event, its purpose and actions that will be taken based on its outcome.

During
- Welcome all participants and thank them for accepting the invitation to be actively involved in the Beta transformation.
- Communicate the opportunities and threats that the organization faces.

- Signal that the work of the meeting is extremely important.
  Words, facial expressions, body posture, tone of voice and authenticity
  are important signals. People throughout the organization are watching for these signals. They indicate how the Sponsor really feels about
  the event and the Beta transformation.
- Introduce the Facilitator and then hand off administration
  of the OpenSpace and get out of the way.
- Participate in the OpenSpace as a peer without coercing
  the other Participants.

After
- Put the Proceedings into everyone's hands as soon as possible, typically by sending an e-mail message with a link to the document. Distribut-
  ing the complete Proceedings quickly indicates that the Sponsor values
  the OpenSpace outcomes and the Beta transformation.
- Call the steering team together to examine and immediately act
  upon the Proceedings.
- Engage in deliberate storytelling that supports the ongoing aims
  of Beta adoption.

It is essential that the Sponsor and other formally authorized managers
continuously signal strong support for the entire process. The best way to
demonstrate executive support is to consider and act, without delay, on the
issues identified in the Proceedings.

{ The Sponsor must really, really be convinced of Beta,
and OpenSpace Beta. He or she must really, really want it:
In effect, no one else than the Sponsor can open the space. }

The Facilitator

According to Harrison Owen, "the key ingredients for deep creative learning are real freedom and real responsibility." The OpenSpace Technology framework creates a safe and open forum where Participants are free to identify, discuss and solve issues that matter most to them. Participants are responsible for making the event successful. The OpenSpace Facilitator's job is to serve the Participants by maintaining or "holding" the space.

The Facilitator is formally authorized by the OpenSpace Sponsor to facilitate and administer the event. Ideally, the facilitator should have no other authority whatsoever within the organization. In turn, the Facilitator formally authorizes the Participants to identify, discuss and solve issues related to the Theme.

The Facilitator prepares the room in advance so that the Participants will have the environment and support they need for creative learning:

- Chairs in a circle facing the middle of the room which is empty except for some blank pieces of paper and markers.
- A large empty wall where session descriptions may be taped or pinned – the agenda will take shape here.
- Posters around the room displaying the Theme, the four principles and the one law, along with reminders to "Be prepared to be surprised."

After receiving formal authorization from the Sponsor, the Facilitator welcomes the Participants, briefly describes OpenSpace and holds the space. The Facilitator provides basic guidance about the mechanics of OpenSpace, explaining the following:

- Any Participant may become a session Convener by proposing and scheduling a discussion about a topic they are passionate about and making sure that the discussion is documented for future reference in Proceedings.
- Participants will be invited to select and attend the sessions that interest them.

- The four principles and the one law.
- "We'll see you all back here for the closing session."

Then the facilitator gets out of the way, expecting, allowing and trusting the Participants to self-organize.

During the rest of the event, the Facilitator does whatever is beneficial to maintain the atmosphere of OpenSpace. This may mean walking around to see what is happening. It may also mean picking up trash and otherwise removing distractions that might interfere with the atmosphere.

At the end of the event, the Facilitator creates the conditions for the Closing Circle and invites Participants to share what they learned - and what actions they plan to take.

The OpenSpace Facilitator should not occupy other roles within OpenSpace Beta, or within the 90 days of Practicing, Flipping, Learning.

{ The Facilitator role is a temporary and silent, but very important role in keeping the space open throughout the OpenSpace. }

The Participants

Participants decide whether to attend the OpenSpace event, its sessions and other conversations.

The OpenSpace Facilitator formally authorizes each Participant to decide how to participate. The facilitator encourages each participant to follow the Law of Two Feet: "If at any time during our time together you find yourself in any situation where you are neither learning nor contributing, use your two feet and go someplace else."

In return, each Participant agrees to be responsible for the success of the event. Participants self-organize to explore aspects of the Theme that they are most passionate about and to share the results of those discussions with the rest of the organization.

Participation in OpenSpace Beta events is completely voluntary. The people who opt in to attend are there because they want to be. This is true regardless of whether they support, tolerate, or resist Beta adoption. OpenSpace gives Participants the freedom to identify, discuss and solve the issues that matter most to them.

Each Participant is free to choose which sessions and other conversations to join. Participants are authorized to become Conveners and propose session topics.

The Conveners

Conveners are OpenSpace Participants who initiate small-group sessions and/or informal discussions. They emerge as nodes of (informal) leadership. Each participant is free to become a Convener by:

- Proposing a topic and adding it to the Marketplace
- Negotiating with other Conveners as necessary to determine where and when the discussion will take place
- Opening the discussion, welcoming the Participants and inviting them to contribute to the discussion
- Ensuring that the results of the discussion are captured and recorded so they can become part of the Proceedings

Convening a discussion means explaining the topic and then keeping the session open for free and open dialogue. It does not mean assembling an audience to hear what the Convener wants to say.

Additional guidelines for each Convener to keep in mind:

- It's okay to discuss a topic in more than one session.
- If no Participants choose to attend your session, you may decide to participate in another session or use the time for personal reflection about the topic – your solutions may end up becoming top priorities.
- It's okay if Participants leave or join during the session – they're just following the Law of Two Feet.

{ Participants and Conveners follow only their own interests and desires. They are thus responsible for their own learning and well-being. }

The four principles of OpenSpace - and the one law

The four principles

Whoever comes is the right people.

Whenever it starts is the right time.

When it's over, it's over.

Whatever happens is the only thing that could have.

(Plus one)

Wherever it happens is the right place.

The one law ("Law of Two Feet")

If at any time during our time together you find yourself in any situation where you are neither learning nor contributing, use your two feet and go to some more productive place.

Part 3

OpenSpace Beta:
Roles & key ideas

(Foundations)

OpenSpace Beta:
Summing it up

OpenSpace Beta is a safe, pragmatic and repeatable technique for rapid and lasting Beta transformation. It works with what you and your organization are currently doing and can be added at any time.

OpenSpace Beta incorporates the power of invitation, OpenSpace, game mechanics, rites of passage, storytelling and more, so your Beta adoption can actually take root. OpenSpace Beta is based on people, then practices. You can use other methods and practices with it - such as Agile or Lean.

Remember: Rapid, effective and lasting Beta transformations are powered by human engagement - not by frameworks, consultants, or coaches!

> You can start using OpenSpace Beta today
> to improve your current Beta organizational model,
> or to get it right the first time.

> Is your Beta, or Agile adoption in trouble?
> OpenSpace Beta can help.

> Just getting started with Beta?
> OpenSpace Beta is the way to begin.

> OpenSpace Beta is *not complicated.*

> It starts and ends in OpenSpace.

> It *engages* people. Big time.

Start and end in an all-hands OpenSpace meeting of at least one day. In-between, implement Beta in a Beta way. Work the system in a way that aligns with and is confirmed by the BetaCodex. This method is iterative and based on self-organization, just as Beta itself. There is a clear beginning, middle and end to each chapter of the transformation.

Key elements
of OpenSpace Beta

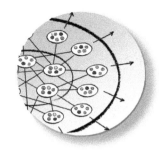

60 days: Build-up (Set stage!) - Part 4 of this book

- Assess the organization's alignment and willingness
  to move towards Beta and OpenSpace.
- Master of Ceremonies: Advise the Sponsor in what to say and do.
- Make sure the Sponsor commits to take immediate action on the
  Proceedings and speaks that commitment to the organization.
- Assure that the Sponsor and other managers generate and tell stories
  that support the overall Beta effort.
- Formally Authorized Managers prepare for OpenSpace Beta.
  They determine the Theme, define a realization period of 90 days
  and explicitly authorize members of the organization to flip the
  organizational model. Managers invite everyone in the organization
  to participate. The intent is to allow everyone to engage.

OpenSpace 1: Beginning (Prepare!) - Part 5

- The first event - called OpenSpace 1 or OS 1 - is an all-hands Open-
  Space meeting. Attendance is 100% voluntary. Everyone at all authorization levels in each affected business unit is invited to attend.
  As a result, there is a huge mixing of people and ideas.
- In the closing circle at the end of OS 1, everyone learns that OS 2 will
  happen in about 90 days. Everyone learns that the organization
  is serious about inspecting results then and making adjustments.

90 days: Practicing - flipping - learning (Do!) - Part 6

- Invite teams to suspend disbelief, to act as if, and pretend that Beta
  principles and practices can work.
- Systematic, intentional, time-boxed flipping towards Beta (interventions on the system are done , including Organizational Hygiene to

remove practices and methods that are in conflict with Beta principles.
- Methods for accelerated learning across the organization are introduced or reinforced.
- Teams understand what they are authorized to do. Then they commit to adapting to BetaCodex principles.
- Encourage practicing, within the boundaries of the BetaCodex principles.
- Formally Authorized Managers engage in deliberate storytelling that supports Beta adoption.
- The teams practice with using any method that align with the BetaCodex´s twelve laws or principles. This is the single firm constraint. There are no others. If a method, or practice obviously offends the spirit of the BetaCodex, it is out of bounds. If a practice does not align with the BetaCodex, it is not a valid practice for practicing during this period.
- Other than the constraints of the BetaCodex and the "90 days", there is no prescription of practices. Teams find practices that work within the boundaries of the BetaCodex.
- Emphasis on learning is reinforced by Formally Authorized Managers: learning what Beta practices are and how to use them in ways that fit the organization´s reason of being, current position and context.
- Ideally, the Formally Authorized Managers also practice Beta practices, such as short daily meetings, iterations and retrospectives. This sends all the right signals and tells a coherent story of transformation.

OpenSpace 2: Ending (Check!) - Part 7

- After the "90 days" of practicing and learning, there is another Open-Space. This all-hands, 100% opt-in meeting is a rite of passage, a look back and a look ahead. One chapter ends and a new one begins.
- The previous chapter is closed and a new chapter of practice opens. By OS 2, teams have unanimous agreement on what is working well and how they want to work. And they start noticing what must change.

- A massive amount of self-organization occurs. The entire organization begins to shift away from command-and-control mediocrity and toward self-organized excellence via continuous improvement.
- The result is huge progress around the entire (invited) group.
- Each 2nd OpenSpace event closes one chapter of learning. It possibly opens another. This cycle may repeat periodically as the organization inspects and adapts.

After completing the first OpenSpace Beta cycle, members of the organization will be thinking much more independently and will be much more responsible for their own learning.

30 days: Quiet period (Level up!) & preparing the next chapter - Part 8

During this "Quiet Period", Coaches and the Master of Ceremonies vacate the organization, learning is digested and deepened, teams find space to "level up".

The last aspect of OpenSpace Beta can be bi-annual OpenSpace events, or "knowledge conferences". Held in January and July, for example, these events are essential. The whole organization anticipates them. They also serve as a cultural initiation for new hires.

Summary

- OpenSpace Beta promotes self-organization and decentralization of decision-making to teams.
- OpenSpace Beta is quite simple - which allows for complexity to emerge.
- It scales. It is not complicated. Each cycle begins and ends in Open-Space. In-between, learning is generated to inform the next cycle of development.

Key elements
of OpenSpace Beta (continued)

- Scale is achieved by the organization itself, by the workforce you already have. Your people become highly engaged and do everything that needs to be done.
- Dependency on expensive and highly paid consultants (who typically have little or no real stake in your future) is greatly reduced.

OpenSpace Beta works for one simple reason: It enables and invites extremely high levels of engagement across your entire organization, potentially. This engagement is essential to the success of your Beta transformation. No other method generates more engagement than OpenSpace Beta does.

OpenSpace Beta is designed to:

- Bring about an organization capable of confronting complex market challenges.
- Create a rapid, effective and potentially lasting Beta transformation.
- Encourage the entire organization to reach a state of self-sustaining, freestanding Beta.
- Save money by reducing the number of consultants and coaches needed to get solid results - and continuous improvement.

OpenSpace Beta works with what you are doing now and can be added at any time.

{ Consistent self-responsibility, self-organization and self-control can be practiced. They must be practiced during OpenSpace Beta, for an organization to sustain a Beta model. }

OpenSpace Beta roles

OpenSpace Beta is a lightweight pattern for empowering and guiding authentic Beta transformation.

OpenSpace Beta has six roles. These roles define boundaries, provide guidance about who is authorized to do what, and open up space for self-organization to occur. There is no coercion in OpenSpace Beta.

- Formally Authorized Managers receive their authority explicitly from the organization. They may assign formal authority to people who report to them directly or indirectly.
  One of them is the Sponsor of the OpenSpace Beta Chapter.

- Influencers & Reputationers receive their authorization informally, from the group or from teams working with-each-other-for-each-other. These people emerge as powerful when members of the group like them, or invite them to take responsibility for what they care about, and they do so.

- Teams include constellations of actors that work for-each-other-with-each-other, practicing Beta patterns.

- The Master of Ceremonies provides reassurance and guidance about "where we are now." This role does not hold any further authority within the organization.

- Coaches model what good facilitation and good patterns of influence/behavior should look like. They are available to provide guidance as it is requested. They are not authorized to force or inflict help.

- Stakeholders or "the further stakeholders" are external actors affected by the adoption of Beta principles and practices. They also benefit from the value that is being created.

The Formally Authorized Managers

Organization charts, job titles and job descriptions formally define position, formal authority and responsibilities for each person in the organization. Formally Authorized Managers have permission to make decisions directing people, policies and money.

OpenSpace Beta requires at least one Formally Authorized Manager: The Sponsor - which is the same person holding the Sponsor role for OS 1. The formally authorized Sponsor must have substantial authority within the organization: This manager must be able to ensure that the first and second OpenSpace events are clearly optional with no formal consequences for opting out. The Sponsor must signal very clearly that OpenSpace Beta is based on invitation and opt-in participation.

Other high-ranking managers with formal authority are tasked by the Sponsor to act on the top ideas in the Proceedings of OS 1 and OS 2. As the Sponsor and formally authorized managers encourage and nurture engagement in OpenSpace, Influencers (those holding informal power) emerge and increase the pace of the Beta initiative and practicing toward high performance.

The Sponsor also guarantees that all practicing, flipping and learning in-between the two OpenSpace events is legitimate.

People watch top managers, especially formally authorized managers. Everyone in the organization will be watching the behavior of these managers. By making their behavior coherent with the organization's intention to achieve high performance and Beta, these formally authorized managers are actively helping write the story of the organization's success.

{ The Sponsor, together with the other Formally Authorized Managers, is in charge of the OpenSpace Beta chapter. At all times. }

The Influencers
& the Reputationers

Positions of formal power include positional authority and account-ability. Formally Authorized Managers are empowered by their positions, within Formal Structure, to make decisions and take actions directing people, policies and money. This power, called hierarchy, is obvious.

Two other, less obvious types of power emerge within every organization:

- One is based on the relationships and interactions between people in the organization. This is *Influence* - and it happens within *Informal Structure.*
- The other is based on mastery, or the capability of solving complex, new problems. This is *Reputation* - which is assigned within Value Creation Structure.

Informal authority, or Influence, is assigned, projected, demanded, declined and withdrawn consciously and subconsciously as people relate. When it feels safe, people accept and embrace the opportunity to become or follow Influencers.
The power of people with mastery, or Reputation, is assigned, projected, demanded, declined and withdrawn consciously and subconsciously as people work together. When it feels necessary, people accept and embrace the opportunity to become or follow Reputationers.

Influencers and Reputationers are the life and blood of OpenSpace Beta. Reputational power helps bring the best ideas directly from the actual contexts where work is being done. Reputationers, or people with repu-tation, are those ideas are based on their mastery and passion for value creation and may not have been seen before.

It can be challenging to allow people take on this critical role. Speeches and policies about employee empowerment seldom do enough to over-come old habits of waiting for permission.

The Influencers
& the Reputationers (continued)

OpenSpace Technology and OpenSpace Beta use Game Mechanics that make it safe for individuals to practice in taking up this role. During each OpenSpace event, everyone in the organization gets to practice with behaving within emergent leadership patterns in the specific contexts they care about.

This breaks the bottleneck that is common to conventional change initiatives: They need to pass back and forth through layers of formal power - and usually never spread out into, or reach the entire organization. Keeping the space open makes sure that everyone can get involved, it dramatically increases engagement and leads to High Performance, fast.

{ Influencers & Reputationers hold power - relational power and the power of mastery, respectively. Ignore these powers at your own peril! }

The Teams

True to the principle of decentralization, Teams in the organization´s periphery are the initial focus of any Beta adoption.
Then come Teams in the organization´s center.

In OpenSpace Beta, teams practice Beta patterns for about 90 days as they tune and adjust their behavior in the direction of continuous improvement.

Teams might range from 3 to, say, 10 team members. 4 to 7 members may be the best sizes. These teams may or may not decide to use specific methods, like Scrum, Kanban or Lean. During the period of practice, flipping and learning, the primary thing that is generated is the learning. All too often there is pressure to get value creation done, even as the teams are figuring out new ways to do so. Yes, Teams are expected to continue to deliver value as they are learning. In OpenSpace Beta, the Teams intentionally choose to try specific practices during the period of practicing, flipping, learning.

You might wonder: "How can all these teams stay in sync if they are each allowed to do something different?"
The answer is surprisingly simple: by periodically (at the beginning and at the end of the Chapter) inviting *all* the Teams and *all* the Stakeholders into OpenSpace. There is no need for central control. When people show up passionate, responsible and fully engaged, the best ideas get heard and the best courses of action are identified and acted upon.

By the time OS 2 approaches, Teams are very aware of what needs to be done for everyone to remain in sync.

{ The main part of the actual work throughout the 90 days is done in the Teams. Here, the thinking, the generation and discarding of ideas, and action-taking on value creation happens. }

The Master of Ceremonies

The Master of Ceremonies is an essential role in the rite of passage event that is OpenSpace Beta. The Master of Ceremonies presides over the passage-rite event, providing guidance about "where we are now". Rites of passage are cultural ceremonies that take individuals and groups of individuals from one "steady state" to another. In between, there is a transition and transformation. Such transitions are often very triggering for participants: No longer "here," and not yet "there," those in a state of ambiguous transition can at times feel very confused.

The Master of Ceremonies helps to maintain the structure and makes sure that the rite of passage is executed well. The Master of Ceremonies is a kind of referee that works in service to everyone who experiences the state of transition (the "Neutral Zone"). In OpenSpace Beta, a single person among the Coaches, never a group or a committee, functions as the Master of Ceremonies during the rite of passage. It is important to note that the Sponsor cannot act as the Master of Ceremonies. This is because the Sponsor is actually a Participant in the rite of passage, together with everyone else.

In OpenSpace Beta, the Master of Ceremonies role is typically occupied by an organizational consultant with a certain level of seniority who is also well-acquainted with OpenSpace Beta (such as an OpenSpace Beta Practitioner).

Throughout a Chapter of OpenSpace Beta, the Master of Ceremonies "coaches" only the Sponsor, the Formally Authorized Managers and those dealing with Proceedings - not other managers, teams or groups. The Master of Ceremonies provides reassurance and guidance through the transition. Somewhat like an orchestra conductor, this individual does not play an instrument, but indicates when tonalities and styles should change, or when to go from *piano* to *forte*.

{ The Master of Ceremonies behaves with prudence, mastery and wisdom. He or she must be perceived as a wise guide and as an encourager - much like Gandalf in a Tolkien novel. He or she is not "in charge", is neither enforcer, nor enabler. }

The Coaches

Coaches model good facilitation and interaction skills.
OpenSpace Beta Coaches invite others to learn these skills.

Each OpenSpace Beta Coach is typically responsible for coaching specific teams, or groups, usually not more than three teams at a time. During the 90 Days of Practicing - Flipping - Learning, Coaches provide facilitation and guidance, and may administer various kinds of before-and-after assessments. These assessments serve as diagnostics and metrics, not for purposes such as judgment or selection.

Several materials at *www.betacodex.org/further-content* can help Coaches to figure out where teams (and the organization) are — and where they can get to next, in a reasonable amount of time.

The Coaching role is about assisting others in learning the Beta principles and patterns, and supporting the execution of practice with specific methods.

When beginning with an organization that is mostly new to Beta, starting with strong momentum is important. This may mean being present almost every day. However, as soon as possible, the Coaches should be absent at least some of the time. For example, after successfully training some employees in using a certain method, it is a very good idea for them to experience life without the Coach for a few days. This helps prepare the Team for when the Coach leaves at the end of the 90 days.

{ The ultimate mandate of the Coach is to help groups or Teams "level up", and take on more and more responsibility for themselves - not becoming dependent on the Coach! }

The Coaches (continued)

Concerning executives

Coaches, in OpenSpace Beta, work closely with Teams, but they must also offer and (if accepted) provide coaching to Formally Authorized Managers with regards to Beta thinking, and help them reflect on behavioral patterns.

Each OpenSpace Beta Coach must pay careful attention to the levels of support among the entire executive team. Strong support from the CEO or other top executives does not mean that everyone on the management team agrees. Some executives can and eventually will work to slow down progress. Beta changes the game for everyone in the organization - not all players will be entirely comfortable with the changes.

The executive team, including the Beta supporters and doubters, may benefit from coaching that is about demonstrating:

- "We executives are learning Beta principles and practicing with Beta patterns and method."
- "We need your skills, passions, abilities and energy to make Beta successful."
- "You are encouraged and free to make suggestions at any level without negative consequences. We will act upon the most important concerns reflected in the OpenSpace Proceedings."
- "We are responsible for high-level organizational direction, decisions and results. You will have free rein to implement some things. You will need to get approval for some things. Some suggestions may not be able to be implemented in this time."
- "We are prepared to be surprised. Surprise us!"

{ OpenSpace Beta Coaches do not "inflict help" on teams, managers or executives. They work closely with those who signal curiosity and strong interest in learning Beta principles & practices. }

The Stakeholders

A Stakeholder is anyone inside or outside the organization who is affected by the introduction of Beta principles and practices. Genuine Beta principles and supporting practices will eventually impact the organizational culture in every dimension. Every member of the organization will be affected by the OpenSpace Beta work and thus is a relevant Stakeholder.

It is thus critically important to invite every member of the organization to the beginning and ending OpenSpace events. OpenSpace Beta makes sure that all affected parties may participate. The organization cannot successfully force Beta or any other transformation upon anyone. What it can do is create fertile conditions for engagement and growth.

The best way to include internal Stakeholders is to invite them to participate in the OpenSpace events. What they do next is up to them.

Because they are part of the market, external Stakeholders (owners, clients, suppliers and others) can provide rich, constructive irritations, too: They provide external reference, as opposed to just internal reference. Without their involvement, the organization will miss significant opportunities for improvement.

{ Stakeholder feedback and engagement are essential. Genuine, authentic invitation is the best way to get it. }

Part4

60 days: Build-up

(Set stage!)

Concepts, context, tasks

This phase is critical to OpenSpace Beta: Without serious preparation work in this phase, nothing can be achieved later. This phase is about focus, about consciousness for the problem and appropriately serious communication efforts.

Concepts

- Assuring that the Sponsor and other Formally Authorized Executives have basic/fundamental understanding of self-organization and Beta
- Using invitation to increase engagement
- Preparing for the first OpenSpace
- Game mechanics

Context

- The Sponsor and other Formally Authorized Executives are confident that Beta and OpenSpace Beta can help the organization solve critical challenges.
- Beta is a different way of thinking about getting work done. Some people in the organization may fear or oppose changing.
- OpenSpace allows people to change without being forced to change. This is very different than issuing mandates.
- The Sponsor and other managers must clearly demonstrate support for practicing Beta, and must clearly authorize the organization to participate.

Tasks

- Craft the Theme for OS 1
- Draft and send the OS 1 invitation
- Hold OS 1 and act on the Proceedings

Power of invitation

OpenSpace Beta is built upon the power of invitation.

Invitation must be "serious". This means two things.
First: Everyone invited must be cherished or wanted.
Secondly: There must be no negative consequences for declining.

The invitation must state clear goals, principles and a rationale for action, so that each recipient can make an informed decision about whether to join.

Issuing an authentic invitation instead of a mandate demonstrates respect for the other person. Respect for people is a core, bedrock value of Beta (as well as Lean, or Agile) principles.

Issuing an invitation is transferring of a small amount of decision-making authority to the individual. When this is done authentically, with no repercussions for opting out, it demonstrates that everyone has an important part in writing the story of the organization's progress.

{ Different than common change management approaches, OpenSpace Beta is a no-nonsense approach to intervention: It relies not on noise, but on calmly producing social density. }

Opt-in participation

As Harrison Owen says: "Without passion, nobody cares.
Without responsibility, nothing gets done."

Passionate and the responsible people who choose to participate can and
will show up to do the hard work of leading the Beta adoption. Allow those
people to opt-in by issuing serious invitations - instead of mandates.

Being invited lets the person control what happens next. It authorizes the
person to decide whether to join the group of people who are writing the
story of the organization's progress.

Feeling a sense of control and a sense of belonging lead to becoming and
remaining engaged. The power of Opt-in Participation, choosing to accept a
genuine invitation, cannot be underestimated.

People who choose to opt in have a high degree of ownership in the outcome. They have an opportunity to demonstrate their passion and take
responsibility to getting things done.
This naturally increases engagement across the organization.

One of the best outcomes of Opt-in Participation is data about whether the
organization is willing to move in the stated direction.

Naturally, the Sponsor will be among the first to publicly and openly opt in.

{ Those who decide for themselves to join
can truly be counted in. }

Preparing executives

The Sponsor, executives and other high-ranking managers must prepare for what will happen during the OpenSpace events and the Beta transformation. Otherwise the adoption will fail.

These managers must communicate extremely well to the entire enterprise before, during and after the OpenSpace events of any OpenSpace Beta implementation.

Preparing executives is an incremental process. Steps include:

- Assimilating and digesting the principles of self-organization and Beta.
- Understanding and accepting the difference between a mandate and an invitation, and the huge differences in the typical results of each style.
- Embracing the OpenSpace meeting format, and their role as Sponsor (host) of these events.
- Engaging in active storytelling before, during and after OpenSpace events.
- Supporting and encouraging informal leadership and allowing them to emerge.

OpenSpace Beta contains a set of guidelines, resources and artifacts – that support the ongoing work of educating the executives as they engage and help write the organization's Beta transformation story.

The executives, and all involved in the change, will experience the challenges of what we call the Neutral Zone (see p. 28). Making use of Coach support, individually and as a team, can shift this phase from frustration to rich learning laboratory. They will also benefit from encouragement, reassurance and advice from the Master of Ceremonies.

{ Executives must understand and accept their unusual role within OpenSpace Beta. That, by itself, is work. }

Coaching role begins

OpenSpace Beta is designed to help organizations learn how to embrace Beta principles as they practice with a Beta organizational model. An essential element of this design is the Coach (or: the Coaching team) whose work it is to:

- Teach the Beta laws, or principles and how to apply them.
- Deliver guidance on specific practices (for example, Compleximeetings, Organizational Hygiene) and why these practices might be useful for a given organization, team or context.
- Deliver specific services to executives and teams, such as meeting facilitation, one-on-one coaching and learning exercises.
- Model good patterns, including respect, adherence to Beta principles, storytelling and Game Mechanics (see next page).
- Identify who is willing to learn new skills. Invite them to enter into a mentored relationship that includes learning by watching, doing and learning via private conversations with the Coach on a day-by-day basis.

The Coaching role begins with Preparing Executives before the first OpenSpace event. It continues through 90 Days of practicing and OS 2. Then the Coaching role ends, as Teams take responsibility for practicing further what they have learned. After the Quiet Period of 30 days, the Coach(es) could begin working with different sets of teams, or they may not return to the organization at all   . A new group of Coaches may then fill the coaching role for the next Chapter, or period of learning.

{ Coaching support is strictly temporary in OpenSpace Beta. It supports through input and know-how about Beta patterns and method, through clarification and accompaniment. }

Game mechanics

In OpenSpace Beta, we hold that happiness at work is best described as a game. And further, that "good games" have "good game mechanics." The best games have clear goals, rules, a visible scoreboard and opt-in participation. The players know why they are there, what needs to be done, and how well they are doing. The fans join in and tell stories about "our" successes and about where "we" need to improve.

These principles also apply to meetings, tasks, projects and initiatives. Every strong game has:

Purpose. Clear goals explain the purpose of the game. In OpenSpace Beta the purpose is continuous improvement and organizational learning by practicing with Beta patterns. Clear goals answer the "why" questions. "Why are we attending this meeting?" "Why are we doing this?" "Why are we doing it this way?"

Principles. Explicit principles inform participants of how they are expected to act and relate to each other towards achieving the purpose of the game. The rules will reflect the values and culture of the game (e.g. competitive, collaborative etc.) It is through the common accepted rules that people feel a sense of membership and belonging in the community of participants.

Feedback. Keeping score of relevant progress metrics (value produced for customers, time to market, sustainable pace, number of defects, cost/income) is what gives teams a sense of progress and accomplishment. With meaningful visible feedback, people can adjust their behavior in order to advance their game and experience a sense of mastery and happiness. Feedback also comes from peer teams, through direct experience and storytelling as the participants write the story of the organization's Beta transformation.

Opt-in participation. Most people want to have some amount of control in their lives. When they choose to participate, they also feel a stronger sense of belonging. A sense of control, feelings of belonging as well as feedback lead to engagement and a strong sense of purpose and responsibility. Opt-in participation is essential. It is an excellent way to avoid the disengagement that often results from coercive mandates.

How to construct a good living system game

Apply Game Mechanics to meetings, tasks, projects and initiatives, to increase engagement, progress and accountability. Strong games produce the best results. The key is to define the initiative in terms of the four components of a good game, and state the principles loudly and clearly. For example:

> The goals are... so that...
>> Our practicing with... is complete. Now we need to decide what to do based on the results.

> The principles are...
>> Be fully engaged in the discussion while you are in the room. If anyone needs to "check out", they may leave the room and return when they can be fully engaged.

> We will measure progress by...
>> Posting the agenda items where everyone can see them and checking off each item as it is complete.
>> Taking a ten-minute break every hour.

> You are invited to participate.
>> Can we all agree to these goals, rules and feedback?

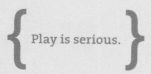

{ Play is serious. }

Setting the stage (60 days)

It takes about 60 days to prepare for the first OpenSpace event and 90 days to organizational Beta. The organization is making a significant commitment by embarking on Beta transformation. True commitment to success begins with proper preparation and socialization throughout the organization.

- The first two weeks (about 15 days) are for Preparing Executives, Theme Crafting, and to Draft/Send an Invitation.

- The next six weeks (about 45 days) are necessary for socializing OS 1.

These time recommendations are for a typical organization that will invite 200 or more people to the event. Smaller OpenSpace Beta implementations may be successful starting with a little less lead-time.
Proper preparation is critical, however. For this reason, 60 days are recommended.

One dimension of the pre-work is creating and sending out the OpenSpace Invitation. When a process-change is being introduced, it is essential for those affected to have enough time to process "what it all means." Be sure to provide enough time for all invitees to examine the Invitation, consider it, discuss it with friends, make travel arrangements, and decide whether to opt-in to living and writing the story of the organization's Beta transformation.

{ Always assume that it takes time to accept an invitation. Accepting an invitation is not and should not always be a spontaneous act. }

Theme crafting

Each OpenSpace event must have a Theme.
The Theme frames the OpenSpace experience.
It serves as a high-level topic.
It indicates the executive group's vision, direction and desire for creative input from all others in the organization. A well-written Theme inspires the attendees to participate in writing the story.

The Theme is crafted in a facilitated meeting convened by the Sponsor. Ideally, the Sponsor invites a sampling of people who represent a cross-section of the organization and they all show up.

The theme is always framed as a question. For example:
- "How can we create an organization of self-organized teams?"
- "Why Beta now?"
- "What must we do to beat our competition?"

The theme must be wide enough to allow space for diverse topics, and narrow enough to provide clear direction about the fundamental topic that needs to be addressed.

The wording of the Theme should also indicate these things in words or in tone:
- Some things are already known ("Why we need to act?")
- Some things are unknown ("How can we best act?")
- Some things are emerging ("What should we do?")

{ The Theme for the first OpenSpace meeting must always be crafted as an open question. }

Draft/Send invitation

People gather together in OpenSpace to discuss topics they are passionate about. The Sponsor is responsible for drafting and sending an Invitation for the event.

The Theme has already been developed and defined. The Theme Crafting meeting generated stories. If a cross-section of the organization participated, positive and supporting stories (signals) about the meeting have been spreading throughout the organization.

The Invitation provides a little more detail about the Theme, but not too much. The Invitation is an opt-in opportunity "to help write the story of the Beta adoption."
The Invitation must be written in a way that the story is not fully defined. The best kind of Invitation omits most of the details. Less is more. The goal is to inspire people to opt in and write the story.

The Invitation should:
- Demonstrate that the event is important to the Sponsor and to the organization.
- Provide just enough information about the Theme and the OpenSpace format so that people will be inspired to join.
- Indicate when the event will happen.
- Provide plenty of time for invitees to respond.
- Make it clear that participation is 100% optional.

Every OpenSpace meeting should be introduced by a genuine invitation, meaning no one is forced to attend. There must be no real or imagined sanctions for anyone who declines.

It is best if the Sponsor writes the Invitation with some help from the Master of Ceremonies, who presumably knows and understand OpenSpace and OpenSpace Beta. The Master of Ceremonies can provide samples and encourage the Sponsor to write something similar in their own words.

Draft/Send invitation (continued)

In all cases the Sponsor should also send the Invitation.
This signals that the event is important, and that responsibility for issuing the Invitation is not being "delegated down."

It is a good idea to leave plenty of time for responding. The invitees need time to carefully consider the Invitation. Many of the people invited may be new to OpenSpace and may be hesitant at first. Allow sufficient time for the invitees to discuss the upcoming meeting, their ideas about the Theme and whether they plan to attend.

In addition to the actual Invitation, it is important to create and distribute different kinds of media, digital and haptic - e.g. leaflets that may be posted in public areas like kitchens, entrance doors and hallways. The Sponsor may delegate the creation and posting of the leaflets. The Invitation and the leaflets, however, must confirm each other and make the event an obvious item to talk about in the days leading up to it.

{ The person sending the invitation determines the weight, and importance of that invitation. }

Socializing the invitation (45 days)

Theme Crafting is complete. The Sponsor has drafted and sent the Invitation to the first OpenSpace meeting.
Preparation continues during the next 45 Days.

- Distribute and post handbills throughout relevant locations.
- Engage in storytelling about organizational learning in the past and the potential for even more learning in the upcoming OS 1.
- Reinforce the fact that participation is 100% opt-in.
- Listen to the stories that members of the organization tell as they talk about the Invitation and what it really means.

The 45 Days should be enough time for everyone to consider and process the Invitation to meet in OpenSpace. People need time to consider the Invitation and decide how to respond. This includes discussing the Invitation with fiends and colleagues inside the organization.

The duration of 45 days is not a strict rule.
In general, the more people you invite, the more time they will need.

{ The power & resilience of Beta organizations lie in the social dynamics they can endure. During the 45 days, this kind of Beta dynamics can for the 1st time unfold and be experienced. }

Part 5

OS 1:
Beginning

(Prepare!)

Concepts, context, tasks

Concepts

- This meeting is a signal event for the Beta transformation.
  To call it a formal kickoff would assume that "not much has happened before", although quite a few things have happened up to this point.
- But when the people in the organization experience this meeting, several crucial things happen: The Participants learn how OpenSpace works. They experience diverse perspectives on the Beta adoption from diverse sources: Teams, executives, managers, directors and Stakeholders.

Context

- The 60 Days of preparation are complete: The Theme and Invitation have been developed, distributed and socialized through the organization. The first OpenSpace meeting has arrived!
- For many participants, OpenSpace will be a new experience. The experience of openness across the entire organization may be a novel experience as well.

Tasks

- The executive team demonstrates their dedication in OpenSpace principles and to acting on the Proceedings.
- During OS 1, the Participants identify and discuss important aspects of the Theme and how to experiment with Beta practices during the next "90 Days". They also learn that OS 2 has already been scheduled.
- This authorizes everyone to suspend disbelief, act as if, and pretend that Beta practices might work while practicing and identifying the best practices. There is no need for mandates.

Day 1. Opt-in meeting: One full day

The first OpenSpace meeting has two important characteristics:

- It must be completely opt-in, meaning it is 100% okay to opt-out, and okay to **not** attend.
- It is best for this event to last no longer than one day.

OpenSpace will be a new experience for many participants. They might be unfamiliar with Beta laws and principles. It will thus take some time for the organization to integrate the learning and experience of the first OpenSpace event. A one-day event keeps it simple, and allows the period of "Practicing - Flipping - Learning" to begin quickly.

The introduction of Beta affects people up, down (outside-in) and across the entire organization. Inviting them to OpenSpace is one way to cross-pollinate these perspectives. The people invited may be hesitant towards the idea of Beta. Or they may be merely tolerating the idea, with a "wait and see" attitude. Others may be strong supporters.

Attendance at the meeting must be opt-in. There cannot be any kind of pressure. Those who do not wish to attend must be afforded the opportunity to opt-out without sanctions.

It is best for the event to include people from various positions and perspectives, people who are genuinely enthusiastic about exploring the Theme of the meeting, as expressed in the Invitation.

OS 2, which follows the 90 days of "Practicing - Flipping - Learning", is announced and socialized throughout the day at this first OpenSpace event.

{ Through the voluntary character of OpenSpace, curiosity, openness and reliability are stimulated. }

Proceedings from OS 1

Proceedings tell the story of the OpenSpace meeting, and help the organization begin writing the story of the transformation.
These Proceedings serve to:

- Share each discussion with everyone in the organization.
- Document the important issues and recommended actions.
- Allow space for Influencers to emerge. They identify themselves and take active roles in writing the story ("our story") of progress into Beta and high performance.
- Make it possible for the Sponsor to fulfill the commitment to act on the recommendations in the Proceedings.

Each Convener takes responsibility for inviting session Participants to contribute to the Proceedings, so that they can share the outcome of their discussion with the entire organization.

- Proceedings contain handwritten or typed notes, diagrams, pictures, lists of session attendees, etc.
- They are collected by one or more Participants who agree to upload them immediately after the session.
- They are shared with the entire organization by a link via e-mail no later than 24 hours after the end of OS 1.

Some Conveners become Influencers in the ongoing process of improvement. Since OS 1 invites participation in the writing of the new story, the session Conveners tend to write the session reports without much help. They do benefit from some direction to ensure that the reports include recommendations as well as a list of attendees. The list of attendees help identify Influencers as well as the people who might be willing to help around specific issues.

The Facilitator of OS 1 needs to support the Conveners and Participants to get the output from their sessions into the Proceedings as soon as possible during the event. This support will include sufficient input devices (e.g. laptops and cameras) at the event, space and tables for those input devices and staff to support the effective use of those devices.

The timeliness of the publishing of Proceedings to all Participants is a critical element of OpenSpace and OpenSpace Beta in particular. The Facilitator sets it up so that the Proceedings are complete very soon after the closing circle, ideally within a few hours. The distribution of the Proceedings should include a message from the Sponsor affirming that the organization will act on the top issues from the Proceedings as soon as possible.

The recommended approach is to for the Sponsor to review the Proceedings and bring the most interested people together to identify, discuss and act on:

- The most important concerns as reflected in the proceedings.
- Recommendations from the proceedings that can be implemented without additional authorization.
- The best recommendations that require additional authorization from the Sponsor, and how to get authorization.
- Recommendations that are beyond the Sponsor's authority.

{ The proceedings create a comprehensive and binding foundation for working the system and value creation after the first OpenSpace. }

Day 2. Prep day: Setting up time-boxed flipping

While the Proceedings are published, or immediately after their publication, Prep day is the moment for setting up the infrastructure needed for "systematically flipping the system towards Beta", throughout the 90 days.

This kind of infrastructure usually does not exist in organizations. So it must be acquired, set up and learned during Prep Day and throughout the beginning of the 90 days. Prep day is supposed to help the Sponsor and other Formally Authorized Managers with setting up this infrastructure, in a public way, and transparent to all. Prep day is not supposed to take the responsibility for the "flipping work" away from the Sponsor and the Formally Authorized Managers.

Participation in Prep day must be 100% voluntary, except for the Sponsor. The Master of Ceremonies should facilitate this day, and the four principles of OpenSpace should be applied to it. For larger organizations, a group of up to 10 people may be needed to do Prep day work. This group cannot resemble a committee, a steering group or task force: It should convene on this day, and then dissolve, to let the Sponsor, the Formally Authorized Managers, the Influencers and the Reputationers do their work during the 90 days.

Prep day will usually start with a complete reading of the Proceedings, followed-up by reviewing, clustering and sorting them, in order to pre-pare for action.

Questions to be asked and discussed during the rest of Prep day include:

- What flips, or intentional interventions on the system (not the people), are identified or suggested?
- What are messages in the Proceedings that might be less obvious?
- What issues must be tackled immediately?
- What are interdependencies between flips? What must be prioritized?

- Who can do it? Who is needed to do the flipping?
- What are the resources needed? How do we secure resources for the flipping work?
- Are there flips that require estimation of preparation times or effort, in order to get them done effectively?
- How should the work of Time-Boxed Flipping be visualized throughout the 90 days, and continuously held transparent (e.g. on a visual board)?
- What kind of additional communication is appropriate, or necessary?
- What methods and additional interventions are we likely to need right away, to accelerate Practicing, Flipping, Learning during the 90 days?

{ Prep day accelerates action after OS 1 and allows to create foundations for the "transformational infrastructure" required throughout the 90 days. }

Part6

90 days:
Practicing - flipping - learning

(Do!)

Concepts, context, tasks

This phase is about systematically acting on the system, in alignment with Beta principles. It is also about disciplined practice with Beta artifacts and patterns - on both the team level and the level of the organization. This must be supported by a learning architecture that accelerates and deepens insight, reflection and continuous improvement.

Concepts

- Aligning teams and the organization with BetaCodex laws, or principles
- Systematic strengthening of value creation, or flow
- Systematic intentional interventions on the system ("flipping")
- Accelerated learning by practicing with Beta patterns
- Deliberate storytelling

Context

- OS 1 revealed several areas that need to be addressed.
- The Sponsor acted quickly on the Proceedings and authorized Teams to select and begin practicing with Beta patterns and "complexitools"
- Managers and Teams need coaching, encouragement and reassurance as they experience new Beta ways of working.
- Nobody is really sure how the practicing will turn out.

Tasks

- Ensure that practices align with the BetaCodex.
- Enable disciplined practicing long enough to understand whether the new practice helps the Team do its work better.
- Allow the Teams to self-organize, so that influence and reputation emerge as Team members learn to act more like teams.

Practicing - flipping - learning (90 days)

90 days, or 13 weeks, is the recommended nominal period of time for practicing Beta patterns in OpenSpace Beta.

A period of 90 days gives the entire organization enough time to gain experience and to figure things out. Less time can work, if it is carefully managed: As few as 60 days can be enough, if the Beta adoption work is well-communicated and well-structured.

The 90 days of Practicing, Flipping, Learning are bounded by OS 1 and OS 2. During these 90 days, executives engage in Deliberate Storytelling, as they encourage practicing with Beta patterns. A Beta pattern is any practice that supports (or does not offend) the 12 laws, or principles of the BetaCodex.

Executives, directors, managers and Teams are encouraged to suspend disbelief, act as if, and pretend that Beta patterns can work, as they practice and learn.

This new learning is pulled into OS 2, where everything is inspected and everyone is encouraged to express what they want, think and feel about the Beta transformation. In this manner, the free and open spirit of Open-Space extends beyond the before-and-after meetings to include the entire 90 days of learning.

Ideally, your OpenSpace Beta work creates fertile conditions for holding "90 days of open space."

{ Mastery arises from disciplined practice.
From thoughtful, method-based, iterative action.
At the same time, the organization is developed. }

Value-creation strengthening

For OpenSpace Beta, and Beta, to leave a mark on the organizational performance and value creation, it is necessary to make value-creating work easier and more likely to happen during the 90 days, and to improve flow.

More effective practices and patterns must be developed, while barriers to team performance must be removed, and waste fought, collectively. We call the practices to be developed Complexitools. Complexitools are organizational methods that are inseparable from human beings: Complexitools are as alive, and as complex as the problems we try to solve with them.

Five areas of focus for working the organizational system will frequently emerge within the 90 days of the first OpenSpace Beta Chapter, in order to strengthen value creation, or organizational effectiveness.
This list of topics here is by no means "complete", but it may serve to focus executives, directors, and Teams on working on the system with maximum impact.

- Practice organizational hygiene: Remove obstacles to performance and barriers to constructive change; remove wasteful tools and dysfunctional practices that inhibit Beta patterns and defy performance. See more on Organizational Hygiene on the next double page.

- Increase transparency: Open the books, make factual information available to all, fast and in the same way to all. Do not allow factual information to be tweaked, or abused. Eliminate "special reports" and individual targets.

- Liberate cell structure: Reduce or remove functional division, integrate functions into mini-enterprises - periphery first, then the center. Decentralize decision-making. Review team constellations and overall structure. Create internal markets with value-creation pricing. Have the periphery retain profits and pay for services provided by the center. Increase resource authority of teams.

- **Introduce relative measures/team reporting:** Liberate reporting systems from planning/forecast data and fixed targets. Create relative (trend) measures/reporting for teams - eliminate all measures below team level (on individuals). Have teams create their own additional performance measures, as needed.

- **Introduce/Strengthen team work methods.** Introduce work method (e.g. from Lean, Agile, Scrum, Kaizen) for teams as needed. Have Coaches provide help to teams, upon demand, to speed up adoption and accelerate and deepen Beta practice. Have Coaches support conflict resolution within teams. Create team working agreements and rituals as needed.

See Part 1 of this book for more about Org Physics, Decentralization and Team Autonomy.

{ Many of the concepts of Beta, and barriers to Beta, may be implicitly known at this point. Now, the challenge is to transform insight into action. }

Time-boxed flipping

The way to work the system on the level of the entire organization, during the 90 days, in order to strengthen value creation, while eliminating barriers to performance, and while fighting waste, is Time-Boxed Flipping.

Time creates boundaries that frame our experiences. Awareness that time is expiring can make it easier for people to suspend their disbelief, act as if, and pretend that new concepts can work. The same awareness can serve as a catalyst for getting things done. Which is why working on Flips, or interventions on the organizational system, should be time-boxed and visualized.

OpenSpace Beta brings about Beta, delivering organizational flips fast, enabling Teams to adapt to Beta ways of working - and at a sustainable pace. During the 90 days between the two OpenSpace events, practicing, flipping and learning are encouraged. Predictable and reliable value creation is the ultimate end goal. This starts with practicing, learning and adoption of Beta practices and patterns. All of this is bounded by time to produce a clearly-marked beginning, middle and end for Participants.

The recommended amount of time between OS 1 and OS 2 is approximately 90 days. A key element to manage is communication about the next Open-Space event. As the organization practices with Beta patterns, it is essential to communicate continuously that results of the practicing will be inspected carefully in OS 2. In practical terms, this means that everyone needs to know the exact date of OS 2. This also means that Formally Authorized Managers (executives) need to communicate the date early and often.

Organizational Hygiene

While all Complexitools may play a role in Practicing - Flipping - Learning, Organizational Hygiene is likely to play a particularly important role within the 90 days. It is often overlooked that the new can hardly take hold in organizations, while contradicting old tools, practices and patterns are left in place. To bring about significant development within an organizations, it is usually necessary to "remove the hand-brakes" present in an organization.

Hand-brakes, here, never refers to people, or individuals, but to practices, tools and patterns.

Contradictory to popular belief, removing tools, rules and patterns is much easier than creating, or introducing entirely new ones. By removing tools, rules, roles and patterns that represent Alpha, organizations and Teams "lift hand brakes" to performance: Space for further engagement and increased autonomy is created; decentralization of decision-making to teams in the periphery is enabled.

Work on Organizational Hygiene, as all work on interventions on the system, should be time-boxed, within Practicing - Flipping - Learning, and visualized and made transparent for all. Deliberate Storytelling plays a particular role in raising the impact of Organizational Hygiene. Time-boxing of the work on flips creates a sense of control over the transformational work undertaken throughout the 90 days.

Tandem meetings

Interaction formats based on self-organization help to maintain the space open, socialize the Flipping and support Deliberate Storytelling. In OpenSpace Beta, a Tandem Meeting is a 90-minute conversational session about the OS 1 Theme, led by a "tandem" of two Formally Authorized Managers, offered publicly for a mixed group of up to 12 people. Participation must be voluntary; the tandem session host constellation changes from meeting to meeting; no decisions are made in a Tandem Meeting, no presentations held, no agenda offered previously. A Tandem Meeting ends after a maximum of 90 minutes. Throughout the 90 days, offer as many Tandem Meetings as possible.

{ Flipping the system, as a Beta way of developing an organization, must not be conducted behind closed doors, but will always be done in plain sight, and actively socialized. }

Learning acceleration

Superior organizational learning is the key competitive advantage for modern-day companies: The increasing complexity and technological advances makes it imperative to leverage the full combined brainpower of teams. When this is achieved, the result should be a collective success for the business.

When there is social density within a team and between teams, then solutions derived from teams are far better than solutions derived by individuals, even the "smartest" among them.

Learning and execution are often at odds in Alpha organizations; learning naturally brings us into the area of unknown and potential defeats, and even occasional failure. In order to facilitate organizational learning, the system has to permit teams to suffer defeats fast – and build upon the learning generated through them.

Organizational learning drives innovation, which impacts the bottom line of a company. In addition, the best talent in the up-and-coming workforce will only consider working in a learning organization with a maximum of self-organization.

People value a networked organizational system, connected without constraint. They value collaboration and getting along over being right. People love collaboration. In order to attract the best people, organizations need to create productive environments where teamwork thrives.

Coaches. In OpenSpace Beta, Coaches serve as a Complexitool for accelerated learning and practicing. Availability of Coaches is time-boxed, as it starts during the 60 days of the Beginning and ends with OS 2. Teams must "pull" support of Coaches.

Learning Circles. Learning Circles devolve learning to teams, or small groups of 4 to 6 members of an organization, to create economies of learning, based on self-organization. Without classrooms, trainings, seminars, teachers, or the boredom of e-learning. This way, the learning becomes learner-driven, and it scales to entire organizations, quickly. Learning Circles are to small groups of learners what OpenSpace is to large groups.

Consultative individual decision-making. Throughout the 90 days, there may be opportunity to practice decision-making not by Formally Authorized Managers, or by group majorities, but by individual Reputationers or Influencers that will be obliged to previously consult those involved with the problem, before making the decision, individually, and for the whole group.

Knowledge conferences. These are gatherings of Reputationers, groups of teams, or "communities of practice" which may be scattered across the organization. Knowledge conferences can be convened during the 90 days to provide cross-fertilization within the organization. They may also be held as gatherings of multiple teams, or clusters of teams. Knowledge-conferences should be highly self-organized and may make use of OpenSpace format.

Counter-intuitively, for Beta organizations, travel is cheap. Beta organizations harvest the power of personal encounters and face-to-face communication - especially for conflict-solving and for removing barriers to performance. Face-to-face communication is paramount to build and sustain social density - something that just cannot be done with emails, chat or any kind of written interaction. Moreover, conference calls of more than three people erode social density. Which is why, in Beta organizations, personal face-to-face conversation, or "picking up the phone to engage in dialog" is highly valued - independent of national culture.

{ The learning in OpenSpace Beta is always equally aimed at the individual, teams and the organization as a whole. }

Practicing
Beta team patterns

In OpenSpace Beta, Teams are authorized and encouraged to practice Beta patterns, and choosing the most appropriate ones. It is best if they then tailor and tune these practices to fit their context, and apply method in a disciplined fashion.

The one constraint is the BetaCodex: Teams are taught 12 laws, or principles of the BetaCodex, and then encouraged to adapt practices that are aligned with this Codex.

The two main outcomes of OpenSpace Beta are high employee engagement and continuous organizational learning. Practicing Beta patterns engages people in direct learning experiences, because they are:

- Confirmed by clear principles (the 12 laws of the BetaCodex).
- Authorized by executives.
- Facilitated and supported by Coaches.
- Celebrated through deliberate storytelling.
- Time-boxed by the 90-day period of Practicing-Flipping-Learning.
- Conducted in the context of current value creation and projects.
- Inspected and adjusted during the second OpenSpace event.

Disciplined team practice in a "flipped system" drives learning

Organizational learning happens when people question the way things are, try things together and make meaning together. Since there is no one way on a team level to "do Beta" but many ways to practice Beta, practicing explores what works and what doesn't for the people and teams involved.

To avoid coercion, or focusing on quickly finding the "right" way to implement Beta (which may result in rigid, sub-optimal practices), everybody should be invited to reflect, share and create situations where learning can take place.

Managers and initiators of new or established practices can emerge and become actors in the organization's story of change and learning.
Some Beta practices are formalized and described in numerous sources, including Lean, Scrum, Kanban, etc. Other Beta practices will emerge as things to try in accordance with the BetaCodex and the organization's purpose, context and situation.

Questioning assumptions behind current practices by asking "Why are we doing this?" and articulating "We must assume x, y and z" is a great way to explore answers to "'What would you do in Beta?"
It is preferable to attack practices and flips of digestible, realistic size and tackle them consistently - instead of attacking big, indigestible challenges, tackled inconsistently.

Anxiety and worries impede learning, as do fuzzy expectations, excessively large challenges, and top-down steering. When skepticism and worries get in the way of disciplined practice, it can be helpful to remind ourselves and others to:

- Suspend disbelief.
- Act as if.
- Pretend these practices can work.

When practicing in a disciplined way, method is applied thoughtfully, nothing is set in stone. All practicing will be subject to inspection and adjustment during the second OpenSpace, where all voices are equally authorized and welcome to speak.

{ Practicing, trying out, varying, practicing again: New team patterns do not emerge out of nowhere. }

The BetaCodex

In order to address complexity, organizations do not need one monolithic theory: They do not need a framework. Instead, they need coherent, shared language and imagery. And a system of systems concepts that everyone in the organization can acquire and integrate, through learning. Consequently, it is crucial to Beta that it is not based on rules, but on principles. Unlike other concepts, the BetaCodex is neither a tool, nor is it a one-size-fits-all solution. It is a system of systems concepts and a mindset. It provides guidance.

The difference between rules and principles is that for setting up rules, you need to analyze every possible situation before formulating it. Rules are based on an "if-this-happens-do-that" logic. Whenever an unknown situation occurs, however, rules fail. Principles, by contrast, do not just apply to known problems. You do not need to be aware of all possible situations. You apply them within whatever situation as it occurs. Understanding this difference, you are able to adopt BetaCodex principles (or "laws") to your organization or to situations you encounter at your work – anywhere, at all times.

Still, it needs some practice to understand the combination of the principles of the BetaCodex. This is because the model is based on a set of 12 coherent and interdependent principles. The principles of the model are not a salad bar to choose from! Only by applying the full set of the 12 principles, organizations will be rewarded with the superior performance the model has to offer.

Since 1998, the Beyond Budgeting Round Table, and later, since 2008, the BetaCodex Network, have drawn upon extensive research and case studies to conclude that there had to be a set of central principles of the organization model based on decentralization and "relative performance contracts", contrasted against the assumptions of centralized command-and-control, plans and fixed performance contracts. This model is based on confidence in teams: Increased transparency and higher expectations (compared to competitors or their equivalent) provide a permanent challenge for teams. Responsibility for performance and decision-making are gradually shifted away from the center of the organization towards the periphery.

Laws of the BetaCodex

Beta is the organizational mind-set that is fit for complex markets
and fit for human beings.
It is articulated through an indivisible set of 12 laws, or principles as follows:

Law	Do this!	Not that!
01. Team autonomy:	Connectedness with purpose,	not dependency
02. Federalization:	Integration into cells,	not division into silos
03. Leaderships:	Self-organization,	not management
04. All-around success:	Comprehensive fitness,	not mono-maximization
05. Transparency:	Flow intelligence,	not power obstruction
06. Market orientation:	Relative Targets,	not fixed, top-down prescription
07. Conditional income:	Participation,	not incentives
08. Presence of mind:	Preparation,	not planned economy
09. Rhythm:	Tact & groove,	not fiscal-year orientation
10. Mastery-based decision:	Consequence,	not bureaucracy
11. Resource discipline:	Expedience,	not status-orientation
12. Flow coordination:	Value-creation dynamics,	not static allocations

2018 version, *www.betacodex.org*

BetaCodex constraints

The 12 laws, or principles of the BetaCodex define the meaning of "Beta" in OpenSpace Beta. There is one essential requirement, or constraint when practicing Beta patterns: All practices must support and align with the BetaCodex. At a minimum, each practice used must not obviously offend any of the 12 laws, or principles of the BetaCodex.

It is a good idea to post the 12 principles of Beta in team rooms and other places where everyone can be reminded of them. Everyone is encouraged to ask questions and insist that practices align with the codex.

Minimal structure during OS 1 and OS 2 encourages Participants to discuss a wide range of topics and ideas. As teams and the organization practice during the 90 days, the BetaCodex provides just enough structure to make sure that they are really using Beta to practice Beta. If the organization follows the 12 principles of the BetaCodex, then each of the answers to the questions below will be "Yes!" Otherwise the practices must be changed.

- Do our current/intended practices support, team autonomy, understood as connectedness with purpose - instead of dependency?
- Do they support federalization, understood as integration into cells - instead of division into silos?
- Do they support leaderships, understood as self-organization - instead of management?
- Do they support all-around success, understood as comprehensive fitness - instead of mono-maximization?
- Do they support transparency, understood as flow intelligence - instead of power obstruction?
- Do they support market orientation, understood as relative targets - instead of fixed, top-down prescription?
- Do they support conditional income, understood as participation - instead of incentives?
- Do they support presence of mind, understood as preparation - instead of planned economy?

- Do they support rhythm, understood as tact & groove - instead of fiscal-year orientation?
- Do they support mastery-based decision, understood as consequence - instead of bureaucracy?
- Do they support resource discipline, understood as expedience - instead of status-orientation?
- Do they support flow coordination, understood as value-creation dynamics - instead of static allocations?

The BetaCodex defines a clear boundary between Beta (encouraged) practices and Alpha, or non-Beta (discouraged) practices. Inside that boundary there is complete freedom for self-organization and disciplined practice. The results can be amazing.

For Beta to take hold in people's minds, interdependencies between the Beta principles must be understood - not just the individual principles. In the context of problem-solving and organizational development, groups should always ask: Which principles (usually more than one) are touched in this situation, and how do our actions affect others? Whom do we have to consult on this?

Consultation ahead of decision-making is the ultimate guardrail, in Beta, for alignment without coercion, for the use of the wisdom of the crowds, without stifling large-group decision-making, or majority voting. Consultative Individual Decision-Making is ideal for Beta organizations: When decisions affect just one team, consultation within each team will be mandatory. When the entire organization or multiple teams are affected, consultation beyond the team of all relevant to the problem is mandatory.

{ Permanent referencing to the BetaCodex throughout the
90 days will help reframe relationships and connections
collectively, anchoring a new mindset in the organization. }

Disciplined practice

During the period between the first and second OpenSpace event, Teams are encouraged to practice with method and patterns – within the "rubber bands" of BetaCodex principles.

With the number of failed or misguided change initiatives in the world of organizations of the last decades, it would be easy to understand if most people came to OpenSpace Beta with a certain amount of scepticism, or even cynicism. OpenSpace Beta encourages executives and Teams to suspend disbelief and practice with flips and learning. When teams see that specific practices they are using actually work, the cynicism slowly fades and Teams begin their advance towards high performance.

Disciplined practice is the key to creating fertile conditions for continuous improvement across the organization. To bring about profound change, individuals need to change their behaviors, and they will do this consistently, once the organization´s system changes. Once we intervene on the system, behaviors will change. This is crucial: People do not resist change, but flawed change methods. Major transitions are nonetheless fraught with stress and fear of the unknown. So hesitation, scepticism and cynicism should be addressed accordingly: Not by blaming, but by clarifying, communicating, providing consequence, and by working on context or the system.

As people adapt to the changed system and figure out how work gets done in this changed environment, they become acquainted with the rules of the game and start considering them "normal". However, when a shift in how work is done is introduced, uncertainty and even fear may naturally follow. Disciplined practice can reduce this anxiety, since nothing is framed as permanent or "set in stone": Changes must be proven to be successful. Without fear and anxiety present, practicing can be run for a specified length of time. Results of practicing encourage new habits and changed behaviors.

{ OpenSpace Beta is not about "creating new stuff", but about applying appropriate method, rigorously. }

Direct experience

In OpenSpace Beta, factual reports and inspection of Direct Experience within Beta principles and practice are valued over logical arguments, debates and differences of opinion. The reason is simple: By the time we finish debating the relative merits of a given approach, we could have completed multiple rounds of practice and received a valuable harvest of Direct Experience.

In other words, some things are better felt than told.

During the 90 days between the two OpenSpace events, Participants are encouraged to conduct as many flips and as much reflected, disciplined practicing of Beta patterns as possible, consistent with the goal of continuous learning and continuous improvement for the organization as a whole.

Most of the people in OpenSpace Beta are problem-solvers. They become highly engaged and discovering and proving solutions to difficult problems. They value specific evidence over exhaustive speculation about feelings, assumptions and expected results.

Direct Experience is "unpacked" during periodic OpenSpace events. During these events, Participants are encouraged to express what they want, think and feel about the use of Beta patterns, Beta principles and related practices. They connect the dots and figure out the best ways to move the Beta transformation forward.

{ Nothing inspires more than solving real-world problems and seeing the results. }

Proprietors of power in action

Formally Authorized Managers are nominated, or *assigned*.
Influencers (those holding power within informal structure)
and Reputationers (those holding power within Value Creation Structure)
emerge.

- Formally Authorized Managers, or those holding power
  in Formal Structure, take care of compliance, or being within the law.
  They try to control engagement, progress, accountability and formal
  authorization of people doing the work, by using formal structures
  such as processes, tools, documentation, contracts, compliance roles
  and communication formats.
- Influencers, or those holding power in Informal Structure,
  take care of people´s need to belong in the organization. They influence engagement, progress, accountability and informal authorization
  of people in the organization, by using informal or invisible structures,
  such as norms, values, culture, stories, group status and relationships.
- Reputationers, which are those holding reputational power within
  Value Creation Structure, take care of the organization´s future results,
  through impacting work and flow of value creation, and solving
  complex problems, within work streams and projects. Through Reputationers, or People with Mastery, the organization discovers hidden
  assets. It develops engagement, progress, responsibility and authorization within the organization by using value creation flow and team
  dynamics. Here, concepts like Invitation, Opt-in participation, Direct
  Experience, stewardship and personal development come into play.

Organizational learning and innovation reveal themselves through emergent leadership, as a person takes initiative and takes responsibility for
team outcomes they are passionate about and would like to try. When it is
safe to suspend disbelief, act as if, and pretend that they can act respon-
sibly, the whole organization learns and discovers hidden value within its
people, teams and value creation structure.

Those holding power in the three structures of the organization have roles to play in encouraging emergent leadership:

- **Engagement:** For emergent leadership to occur and for people to assume more responsibility for organizational and team results, they have to be invited to do so. Any perceived risk for stepping up will prevent people from trying, so there can be no formal assignment within Formal Structure, and no informal assignment or peer pressure from Teams within Value Creation Structure. Invitation means anyone can accept and decline, regardless of formal title, influence or mastery.
- **Progress:** Progress during OpenSpace Beta is measured through stories about initiatives, unfolding Beta patterns, emergent leadership and direct learning experiences. Formally Authorized Managers need to communicate and celebrate stories of safe space learning efforts, regardless of the outcome. Influencers need to connect, and strengthen those taking responsibility. People with Mastery need to support and encourage those challenging their own learning edge.
- **Accountability:** People with reputation step up because they want to sharpen their alignment of purpose, autonomy and mastery. They say: "I want to make this happen." People with Mastery feel accountable to a work-related organizational purpose, and to their Team´s sense of autonomy and mastery, by promoting learning. Formally Authorized Managers emphasize accountability through contracts and agreements. Influencers emphasize relationships.
- **Authority:** Formally Authorized Managers authorize work through formal approval, thus creating conditions for change and value creation. Influencers do so by socializing change, agreements and conditions for flipping. Reputationers emerge by assuming responsibility for work and results, and by responding to the reality of market-pull. Emergent Leaderships authorize anyone to emerge as taker of responsibility, and maker of decisions. Responsibility must be authorized within Formal, Informal and Value Creation Structures: "May I assume responsibility for this initiative?" is an invitation that can be accepted or declined.

Deliberate storytelling

Part of the culture of an organization is created and reflected by the stories told by its people. Stories about the past, the present and the future help create a coherent, or incoherent narrative of who and how the organization is. The life of the organization is made alive through the telling and retelling of these stories.

When an organization and its people are going through change, the need for stories is elevated. People naturally look to those with power(s) to fill this gap. If Formally Authorized Leaders, Influencers, or People with Mastery fail to provide coherent narratives about change, the people will create stories themselves, to make sense of the changes they experience. When stories are generated from reaction rather than intention, the stories may or may not support and align with the overall purpose of the change. When this happens, the organization risks creating a culture based on random, incoherent stories that do not align with organizational goals. This creates completely unnecessary and counterproductive levels of confusion, resistance, and fear.

Those holding powers within the organization can fill this void with deliberate storytelling and intentional story generation. Successful organizational change happens when the purpose of change is communicated through coherent storytelling of Formally Authorized Managers, Influencers and Reputationers. Storytelling begins before the first OpenSpace event and continues through the practicing with Beta patterns and OS 2, and carries on into the future as the organization continues to develop.

Past, present, and future

Telling positive stories about the past honors the people who participated in previous successes. It creates a coherent narrative by identifying strengths from the past that can create positive outcomes now.
Since all change happens in the present, it is here that stories of disciplined

practice, flipping and learning can be shared: Who is trying what, and what is the outcome? These stories speak to the nature of going through change by creating lots of learning through practice.

Stories about the future are visions. These stories will inform how present activities will lead to future ways of working.

Story generation

Telling stories about the past, present and future helps create the coherent narrative of the flow of changes within the 90-day Rite of Passage. By engaging in deliberate, authentic actions and behaviors, members of the organization can generate stories about organizational change.

To generate stories, those with power in the three structures of the organization must intentionally behave in ways consistent with the change story, and leave the storytelling to whoever will pick it up. For example, whatever Formally Authorized Managers pay attention to will signal importance to the rest of the organization.

We navigate the world via signs and signals. In organizations, people look to those with power to help make sense through change. Those with power provide signals about where we are and where we are going. Inside OpenSpace Beta, those with power should be conscious to integrate the idea of signaling into everything they do: People tell stories about behavior of those with power!

{ Through intentional, Deliberate Storytelling, organizational interventions are more likely to "take root" and have maximum impact on communicative patterns and the system. }

Part 7

OS 2:
Ending

(Check!)

Concepts, context, tasks

This phase is about Ending the Beta transformation phase of 90 days, and about checking, or reviewing and making sense of the experiences.

Concepts

- Preparing for the second OpenSpace
- New Theme and Invitation
- What should the organization do next?

Context

- The Teams have experienced OpenSpace, so they know what to expect with OS 2 and self-organization.
- The Teams have gained Direct Experience from practicing with Beta patterns for about 90 days. They have seen what worked and what did not, and they have learned how to align their practices with the BetaCodex.
- Time is running out. The Coaches will depart soon. It is time for the Teams to level up and take responsibility for moving the Beta transformation forward.
- OS 2 serves as a rite of passage as the current chapter of learning closes and a new chapter begins.

Tasks

- Craft the Theme for OS 2
- Draft and send the OS 2 invitation
- Hold OS 2 and act on the Proceedings

Theme & invitation for OS 2

Theme & Invitation are critical components in planning and preparing the organization for each OpenSpace meeting. Before OS 1, the Invitation introduced OpenSpace, the Beta transformation and the Theme, along with the importance of Opt-in participation.

Toward the end of the 90 days of practicing Beta patterns, the organization will be expecting OS 2. And, in general, the people who plan to attend this will be well-prepared for it. OS 2 functions as an organization-wide retrospective.

The story of the shifts that happened during the previous 90 days will be fresh in their minds. They know about Proceedings and how quickly they will be distributed and acted upon. Active, Deliberate Storytelling during the previous 90 days has been confirming and supporting the ongoing process of practicing, flipping and learning.

There is also an emergent awareness of the most difficult obstacles facing the organization and the goal of continuous improvement. People are aware of the upcoming Coaching Role Change, and the time-boxed availability of the Coaches.
Time is running out.

In helping the Sponsor craft the Theme & Invitation for OS 2, the Coaches and Master of Ceremonies can change tactics and speak more directly. Their roles will change soon. They can "sharpen their rhetoric".

OS 2 will be less novel and tend to have lower attendance. However, those who do participate will be better prepared and ready to tackle clearly identified issues with greater focus and commitment.

{ The OS 2 Theme must be even more edgy, and more gripping than that of OS 1, in order to focus development. }

Second OpenSpace meeting (OS 2)

The second OpenSpace event will be different than OS 1.

- Everyone knows how OpenSpace works now.
  The original novelty of OpenSpace is no longer present.
- It is not just a prospective meeting looking forward,
  it is also a retrospective looking back.
- Everyone has observed and experienced how Formally Authorized
  Managers behaved after OS 1 and during the 90 days.
- Some who were originally resistant may have become
  more tolerant of the proposed changes, or even supportive.
- Tolerators may now support Beta transformation.
- Everyone has a very good idea of where everyone else stands
  with respect to the process of practicing Beta patterns.
- The easy-to-remove impediments are mostly dealt with
  and some very thorny problems and issues remain.
- Those who are prone to "gaming the system" are likely
  to be conspiring about how to "play" and participate in the OS 2 event.

The Sponsor can harness this energy by focusing on removing obstacles
described in the Proceedings.

So here is what you can expect:

- Lower attendance, overall. OS 1 attendance included
  some curiosity seekers. They tend not to attend OS 2.
- The topics tend to be much more focused on a few big issues -
  the things that are holding back the next level of progress.
- The closing circle is smaller.
- The Coaches are leaving or otherwise shifting their role
  to a substantially new role, for example: Shifting from coaching Teams
  to coaching just executives, product owners, facilitators and Scrum
  Masters. Or shifting from "whole systems coaching" to one-on-one
  coaching.

The OS 2 event is an important inspection point. During this meeting, the organization inspects the outcome of the last 90 days of practicing Beta patterns. Practices or method that are not clearly working are adjusted, tailored, or even discarded as a result of discussions inside this meeting.

In the context of OpenSpace Beta, the purpose of OS 2 and the following Quiet Period is to:

- take stock of the learning.
- integrate the learning and make sense of it.
- pause long enough to be stable in the learning - by building a foundation and basis for further learning.

Impediments to continuous improvement tend to be clearly identified and discussed.
Which is why OS 2 is also a call to action.

The OS 2 event also has a high concentration of people who are truly committed to continuous improvement and getting to high performance. The people who attend OS 2 are the people who like the very open approach – and the very strong results – of OpenSpace Beta.

{ In OS 2, it becomes clear what is possible, and what isn´t yet. }

Day 1 & 2: Opt-in meeting

The second OpenSpace meeting (OS 2) is a great place to define and execute actions. The group has experienced OS 1 and 90 days of practicing Beta patterns. The group as a whole knows the issues, the opportunities and the problems.

Individual members of the organization have a very good idea about who is currently supporting the process of change – and who is not.

For these reasons, OS 2 may be a longer meeting. A two-day event allows time for identifying issues, solving problems and taking action. On the other hand, a Prep Day (as in OS 1) will not be necessary, as the infrastructure for Time-Boxed Flipping already exists. The Participants can move to action immediately in a way that extends beyond the Formally Authorized Managers to include everyone present.
OS 2 is about sharpening focus, intentions and results. It is about taking action.

An excellent way to sequence OS 2 is to start it on the afternoon of the first day, and continue for a full second day. This slightly wider period of time can include activities at the end that create energy, action and increased momentum on the issues that are most important to address and to solve.

During the last part of the second day, the Facilitator can include activities to encourage ownership of and action on the issues that are holding the group back. The 90 days are over and people are feeling empowered.
So OS 2 is a great place for Formally Authorized Managers to signal that the group has enough authorization ("permission") to take up the leadership of the Beta adoption and achieve Increased Momentum for themselves.

{ OpenSpace 2 makes first results visible and experienceable.
The work gets more focused. }

Proceedings from OS 2

The Proceedings for the second OpenSpace event (OS 2) serve many of the same functions of the Proceedings of OS 1, and require most of the same support.

But there are significant differences:

- People understand the process and require less direction and hand-holding.

- OS 2 usually has a smaller but more determined attendance. Those who do attend typically show up with a much higher level of commitment and focus.

- The topic list is shorter and tends to focus on the biggest obstacles and impediments in the way of a high performing and learning organization.

- A Prep Day will not be necessary, as the infrastructure for Time-Boxed Flipping already exists.

- A similar post-OpenSpace inspection meeting happens, but the current role of the Coaches ends for the Quiet Period, after executives inspect the OS 2 Proceedings. The Master of Ceremonies may sharpen his/her rhetoric, in anticipation of the change in, or end of his/her role. The Proceedings of OS 2 are a rich source of material for the sharpened rhetoric: With these proceedings, the Master of Ceremonies can underline critical items for executives to heed.

After OS 2, the focused and committed emergent leadership will tend to experience the Coach-role change as a signal to "step it up". They now understand what needs to happen to "level up."

{ The proceedings become more sophisticated and complex, content-wise. Quality matters more than quantity. }

Part8

30 days:
Quiet period

(Level up!)

Concepts, context, tasks

This phase is about deepening the Beta experience and about digesting the transformation work.

Concepts

- One chapter ends, another begins
- Reflect, inspect and adjust behavior
- Recurring OpenSpace

Context

- This chapter of Organizational Learning is complete. Issues emerged in OS 1. Executives acted on those issues and authorized Teams to conduct practicing, flipping and learning during a specific window of time.
- The most engaged people attended OS 2 and identified the remaining big issues. Executives acted on Proceedings and authorized the Teams to proceed.
- The people have experienced self-organization, control, and they have a sense of progress as they graduated to a new level.

Tasks

- Change the role of the Coaches
- Debrief the OpenSpace Beta chapter.
- Schedule the next recurring OpenSpace, if appropriate

Quiet period
(30 days)

The second OpenSpace meeting is a closure event. It establishes the boundary between the previous chapter of Organizational Learning and the potential next one. It is the final point in the organizational rite of passage. For the rite of passage to be most effective, the organization must have a sense of "leveling up", or graduating. It is okay if, with this leveling up, the Beta transformation stops here.

We call these 30 days the Quiet Period. The Coach(es) should vacate the organization for at least 30 days following OS 2. Doing so promotes a strong sense of progress and moving to the next level. It supports feelings of graduation. If the Coaching role does not change between chapters, there will be a diminished sense of progress. So the role must change. The goal of OpenSpace Beta is to bring the organization to a state of self-sustaining, freestanding Beta as soon as possible. For this to happen, the Coach's role and perceived authority within the Teams must diminish.

The 30 day period following OS 2 is a time for the people to integrate their learning from OS 1, from Practicing - Flipping - Learning, and OS 2. It is a time to reflect on what they have learned, to inspect the results and to tune and adjust their behavior.
This is a good time to ask some questions including:

- How rapidly has the organization acted on the Proceedings from OS 1 and OS 2?
- Is the organization making substantial changes?
- What are the results of the initial 90-day practicing of Beta patterns?
- What kinds of actions is the organization taking without being directly prompted by the Master of Ceremonies or the Coaches?
- What is happening in terms of people, plans and policies, as a result of OpenSpace Beta?
- Have the teams learned to tailor practices to align with the BetaCodex, in order that they might do their work better?
- Have champions for the transformational Beta change emerged?
- Can you identify them by name?

Energy, action
and increased momentum

By the time the second OpenSpace event approaches, people are energized and ready to take action. They have practiced Beta patterns in an open environment. During OS 2, they look back and they look forward to the next phase of escaping from patterns and practices that did not work.

Encourage and initiate action inside OS 2 rather than waiting for Formally Authorized Managers to act in a certain way. This is the time and place to encourage even higher levels of engagement and commitment. Wise Formally Authorized Managers can direct that energy as they signal the areas in which the group is empowered to take action.

OS 2 is typically characterized by three or four big issues that stand in the way and need to be resolved. There may be a need for product roadmapping at the enterprise level. Or there may be existing policies or roles that need to be amended or completely abolished, because they stand as impediments to continuous improvement. There will be problems that are big, that need attention, and require action: It is likely that Organizational Hygiene must continue.

To address these issues and maintain forward momentum, it is best to encourage problem-solving action inside OS 2. The Master of Ceremonies, the OpenSpace Facilitator and the Sponsor should work together to architect some activities inside this meeting that will strongly encourage action on and ownership of problem-solving.

It is imperative that all of this is duly authorized by the Sponsor.

Ideally, this is the state of being for the organization after OS 2:

- The group can clearly identify the top issues of immediate concern.
- Each issue has a champion who brings passion and responsibility to the task of addressing and solving the problem.
- Each issue has a wider team who pitch in to help.

- For each issue, the champion and the team have very clear agreement about who is doing what to address the issue after OS 2. In this manner, a sense of progress across the entire organization begins to manifest.

Before long, the system starts to move in the direction of continuous improvement and a strong intention to create great results. When this happens, many impediments tend to go away entirely, as those who are not really supporting the Beta transformation realize that more than a few things have changed in the past 90 days. The organizational system is actually shifting and approaching the Increased Momentum it needs, in order to continue moving forward.

{ During the 90 days, results are not guaranteed. Clarification, however, is guaranteed. It becomes clear to anyone who is willing to see, what is possible at the given moment. }

Coaching role ends

One of the core ideas that OpenSpace Beta is built upon is that people feel good when they experience a sense of progress. In gaming, "leveling up" delivers a sense of progress. In standard change initiatives, the same coaches might stay with a team or the organization for years.
This becomes an impediment for teams that are looking for a sense of progress and specific events that demonstrate progress.

In OpenSpace Beta, a segment of learning bounded by two OpenSpace events is called a Chapter. Each Chapter represents a passage, and specific progress. The role of the Coaches changes formally at the end of each Chapter. It is essential that the role of Coach diminishes with each Chapter that starts and ends in OpenSpace. The reduction in the authority of Coaches has a symbolic and a practical aspect. In practical terms, the Teams must know that their Coaches cannot be depended upon to answer all questions forever, and that they must mature to the point where they need little (if any) coaching to continuously improve. In symbolic terms, the reduction of the authority of Coaches means that Teams are assuming at least some, if not all the authority Coaches originally started with.

In OpenSpace Beta, Coaching is strictly time-boxed. During the 30 days after OS 2, Coaches are required to "go away" for at least 30 days. By vacating for 30 days and creating at least a small vacuum, the organization should get encouraged to get busy without help from an external authority (the Coaches and the Master of Ceremonies). Announcing the fact that the Coaching role is going to change as of OS 2 is an essential aspect of OpenSpace Beta. This announcement signals that the Teams and everyone else involved need to get busy assuming more and more responsibility for moving the Beta transformation forward.

Coaches must continuously reaffirm that their role is entirely temporary in nature. Coaches must communicate to the executives, directors, managers, and Teams that they must begin the challenging (and rewarding) process of learning how to reach a state of freestanding and self-sustaining Beta for themselves. This means being able to continuously improve, without the need for an external authority telling them what they "should" do.

When organizations make progress with flipping, and when people adapt to changing systemic context, there will be need for some amount of coaching along the way. But the organization as a whole needs to feel a sense of progress, too, as it closes the previous chapter of organizational learning and begins a new one. The Coaches may have been perceived as authoritative figures ("external reputationers") in the previous chapter. But when the Coaches vacate that role and move on to work with other Teams or in other organizations, the Teams cannot help but level up - and begin writing the next chapter of their Beta transformation story. New mandates for Coaching may later be given, of course: Coaching may continue in the new chapter, with the same or different Coaches. The entire purpose of shifting the role of Coaches with each chapter, however, is to deliver a sense of "leveling up" and progress as the entire organization writes its transformation story. Periods of organizational learning are framed by OpenSpace events that serve to punctuate the end of one Chapter and the beginning of another.

The OpenSpace events are important rituals, rites of passage or ceremonies that define boundaries by time and experience. This is like the progression of ceremony and ritual we know from our school years: As we progress through the grades, graduation ceremonies punctuate the end of one chapter and the beginning of a new one. So it is with OpenSpace Beta. With each OpenSpace event, the authority of Coaches decreases formally. This delivers a periodic and strong sense of progress across the organization. Without this change of status of Coaches, there is no progress, and in fact no passage "from now to new."

{ The entire job of the Coaches is to get Teams and the organization, to a state where members of the organization themselves are taking total responsibility for their own learning. This does not happen all at once. }

Higher performance

Organizations use OpenSpace Beta with intent to create Higher performance. Higher performance emerges team by team, as the transformation progresses.

Enough structure is provided to allow Teams to apply different Beta practices and patterns, with the ultimate goal of finding the set of Beta practices that accelerates performance.

Once team members experience the power of autonomous decision-making regarding how they work, they begin to sharpen their ability and motivation to sense areas in need of attention. This increased engagement leads to even higher performance.

When a Team hits its stride, the positivity is infectious. When this happens in a sufficient amount of Teams, after a while, the entire organizational system starts to re-focus on continuous improvement. When this happens, the culture will be truly shifting.

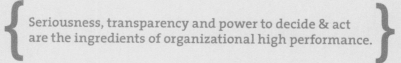

{ Seriousness, transparency and power to decide & act are the ingredients of organizational high performance. }

Chapter debrief

After the Quiet Period of 30 days, the Master of Ceremonies reviews, together with the Sponsor, the chapter results and experiences. A debriefing occurs, which serves the purpose of "Chapter supervision". This is the moment for more subtle patterns and paradoxes from the entire chapter experience to be reflected upon and to be reviewed critically by the Sponsor.

The Master of Ceremonies, just as the Coaches, vacates the organization and does not communicate with it for at least 30 days, during the Quiet Period, to trigger self-sustaining self-organization behaviors on the part of the client organization. The Chapter Debrief finalizes the Master of Ceremonies role within the chapter.

Based upon the Chapter debrief, the Master of Ceremonies, may deliver specific coaching on what to (possibly) consider next. The chapter debrief itself will focus on topics and aspects for evaluation and reflection, such as the following:

- Echoes from the 90 days and from the 30 days of the Quiet Period.
- Evaluation of the energy level(s) before and after the OpenSpace Beta chapter, within the organization, and in different parts of it.
- Recognition of patterns old & new -
  and interpretation of their meanings.
- Consequences for further work on the system,
  and further action by teams on their value creation.
- Personal learning of the Sponsor.

There may be an additional debriefing session, or format, together with all Formally Authorized Managers.

{ What have we learned during the entire OpenSpace Beta chapter? That question is at the heart of the Chapter Debrief. }

Recurring OpenSpace

Each OpenSpace Beta Chapter creates a rite of passage that begins and ends with an OpenSpace meeting. What happens after that?

In Open-Space Beta, this pattern of the rite of passage may become periodic, and thus part of the system, and the "culture". A key feature of OpenSpace Beta is the possibility of institution of periodic and recurring OpenSpace meetings.

In practical terms, members of the organization are likely to think much more independently after the first OpenSpace Beta chapter, and are much more responsible for their own learning. A decrease of the Coaches' authority is essential and must be emphasized throughout the rite of passage process, to underscore the fact that the organization is making progress integrating Beta patterns into the organization's system. In the end, a Beta organization should become able of running OpenSpace Beta chapters independently of external help.

The additional aspect of ongoing OpenSpace Beta can be the biannual Open-Space meeting. Held in January and July, for example, these events may play an important and essential role: The whole organization will anticipate them. They are cultural ceremonies or rituals. They also serve as a place for initiating new hires into the system's organizational learning & development.

The fixed scheduling of these events forms a capsule for the learning and the Neutral Zone experiences that come with it. These "work the system" events support the continuous learning that any Beta organization must create.

By including these recurring *work the system* events on the organization's calendar, the risk of dependency on any one leader is greatly reduced and might even be eliminated. This is of particular importance to organizations in perpetual Beta. A typical failure pattern in the adoption of Beta occurs when a highly authorized Sponsor and progressive executive exits the company. The space necessary to do Beta may well depart with that executive.

Instituting recurring semi-annual OpenSpace events provides a framework for continuing the Beta transformation forever, regardless of whether previous Sponsors are still with the organization.

{ OpenSpace Beta offers the opportunity to become a strong ritual for the organization, and part of the organization's culture. }

The rest

Additional resources & more

(Useful stuff for Beta work)

Recommended reading

Social dynamics, OpenSpace & Prime/OS

Denning, Steven: The Leader´s Guide to Storytelling – Mastering the Art and Discipline of Business Narrative. Jossey-Bass, 2005

McGonigal, Jane: Reality is Broken – Why Games Make Us Better and How They Can Change the World. Penguin Books, 2011

Mezick, Daniel: The Culture Game – Tools for the Agile Manager. FreeStanding Press, 2012

Mezick, Daniel/Pontes, Deborah/Shinsato, Harold/Kold-Taylor, Louise/Sheffield, Mark: The OpenSpace Agility Handbook. New Technology Solutions Inc., 2015

Owen, Harrison: A Brief User´s Guide to OpenSpace. Available on: *www.openspaceworld.com/users_guide.htm*

Owen, Harrison: OpenSpace Technology – a user´s guide. Berrett-Koehler Publishers, 2008

Owen, Harrison: Spirit – Transformation and Development in Organizations. Free pdf: *www.openspaceworld.com/spirit.pdf*

Owen, Harrison: Wave Rider – Leadership for High Performance in a Self-Organizing World. Berrett-Koehler Publishers, 2008

Turner, Victor: From Ritual to Theatre – The Human Seriousness of Play. PAJ Publications, 2001

Turner, Victor: The Ritual Process – Structure and Anti-Structure. Aldine Transaction, 1995

Beta & BetaCodex

Haeckel, Stephan: Adaptive Enterprise – Creating and Leading Sense-And-Respond Organizations. HBRP, 1999

Pflaeging, Niels: Organize for Complexity – How to Get Life Back Into Work to Build the High-Performance Organization, BetaCodex Publishing, 2014

Pflaeging, Niels/Hermann, Silke: Complexitools – How to (re)vitalize work and make organizations fit for a complex world. BetaCodex Publishing, 2018

Pflaeging, Niels/Hermann, Silke: Org Physics - Explained, BetaCodex Network white paper No. 11, *www.betacodex.org/white-papers*

Purser, Ronald/Cabana, Steven: The Self-Managing Organization – How Leading Companies Are Transforming the Work of Teams for Real Impact. Free Press, 1998

Seddon, John: Freedom from Command and Control – Rethinking Management for Lean Service. Productivity Press, 2005

Organizational development, learning & change

Bridges, William: Managing Transitions – Making the Most of Change. 25th anniversary edition, Da Capo Lifelong Books, 2017

Deutschman, Alan: Change or Die – The Three Keys to Change at Work and in Life. Harper Business, 2007

Kleiner, Art: Who Really Matters – The Core Group Theory of Power, Privilege, and Success. Currency/Doubleday, 2003

Kotter, John: Leading Change – With a New Preface by the Author, 1R edition, HBRP, 2012

Kotter, John/Rathgeber, Holger: Our Iceberg is Melting – Changing and Succeeding Under Any Conditions. St. Martin's Press, 2006

McGregor, Douglas: The Human Side of Enterprise. Annotated edition, McGraw-Hill, 2005

Morgan, Gareth: Images of Organization. Sage Publications, updated edition, 2006

Weisbord, Marvin: Productive Workplaces – Dignity, Meaning, and Community in the 21st Century, 3rd Edition. Pfeiffer, 2012

Complementary online stuff & video content

Bonus online content: Additional resources are available on the extras page of this book´s website at: www.OpenSpaceBeta.com and on www.betacodex.org

Videos on Beta and OpenSpace Beta

Watch online videos about **Beta and the BetaCodex**

Watch online videos by the authors about **OpenSpace Beta**

Videos and more on OpenSpace and Prime/OS

Watch online videos on **OpenSpace Technology** with Harrison Owen

Watch online videos with Daniel Mezick about **OpenSpace Agility**

Visit the **Prime/OS** website

BetaCodex Network resources

Read the **BetaCodex Network white papers**

Read **articles** recommended by the BetaCodex Network

Check out the list of recommended **books on Beta**

Other books by Silke & Niels from BetaCodex Publishing

Volume 1

Volume 2

Niels Pflaeging
Organize for Complexity.
How to get life back into work to build
the high-performance organization
BetaCodex Publishing,
Paperback/eBook, 2014
ISBN 978-0991537600

Also available in German,
Portuguese, Turkish
www.organizeforcomplexity.com

Niels Pflaeging I Silke Hermann
Complexitools.
How to (re)vitalize work and make
organizations fit for a complex world
BetaCodex Publishing,
Paperback/eBook, 2018
ISBN 978-0991537679

Also available in German.

www.complexitools.com

www.betacodexpublishing.com

About Silke Hermann

I am an entrepreneur and a business-woman. A colleague once said that, most of all, I am a business humanist. Until recently, and for more than ten years, I was a general manager and owner of Insights Group, a learning and development service firm in Germany with offices in Berlin and Wiesbaden, and with roughly 25 people. With selling my shares in Insights, new opportunities of development that I have wanted to pursue for a while opened up.

OpenSpace Beta is my fourth book. My previous books include Complexitools, which I wrote together with Niels and which sold 18.000 copies so far in German alone. Recently, I also wrote a pocket guide on personality types. For me as an author, writing this handbook has been special, though: OpenSpace Beta brings together several threads of activity that are of interest to me. Niels and I have been developing consulting approaches for Beta transformation since early 2009, when we started working together on client projects. Early Beta projects involved a law firm and a large bank. In this context, we employed John Kotter´s *Leading Change* concepts and *OpenSpace* with our clients, among other methods. But something was missing. With hindsight, I can say that it is the insight that Beta transformation *cannot be done by, or with consultants*. The radically new thing about OpenSpace Beta is that it combines the goal (Beta) with radical self-organization by the client, and, in fact, no need for consultants at all. To anyone who has struggled with organizational transformation for so long, this is a very big deal!

Niels and I recently founded Red42, a company that is set to disrupt organizational transformation and Learning & Development in organizations as you know it. With Red42, we are strictly dedicated to highly innovative, even disruptive approaches to Learning & Development - OpenSpace Beta being one of them. At the same time, we are launching Learning Circles by Red42, which make workplace learning available to all in organizations - without the need for seminars, classrooms, trainers, experts, or elearning. More about what Red42 is doing can be explored on *www.RedForty2.com*.

I look forward to hearing from you. Get in touch, if you like!
E-mail: silke.hermann@redforty2.com. Follow me on Twitter: @SilkeHermann

About Niels Pflaeging

I am an advisor and a speaker. I like to think of myself as a serious business thinker, but at the same as a practitioner who gets the nitty-gritty details of business. As an advisor, I have been helping organizations of all kinds to master profound change, for 15 years now. From 2003 to 2007, I was a director of the *Beyond Budgeting Round Table (BBRT)*, the think tank that developed the foundational research into what we now call *Beta*, or the *BetaCodex*.

Before my time with the BBRT, I worked as a finance manager at multinational companies. But it was during my time with the BBRT that I discovered my passion for organizational transformation towards coherent self-organization. In 2008, I co-founded the *BetaCodex Network*, the open source movement for Beta transformation. You can find more about Beta and about the network on *www.betacodex.org*.

By the time my second book, Leading with Flexible Targets, was published, back in 2006, we at the BBRT understood that explaining the new, better organizational model would not suffice to change the world of work: We also had to solve the riddle of how profound and organization-wide "transformation" could be pulled off! I believe that, with OpenSpace Beta, this riddle has now been solved.

This is my 7th book about organizational transformation and the third book I wrote with Silke. This one stands out in that it is "just a handbook" - no more, no less! To Silke and me, the creative act of transforming Daniel Mezick´s original *OpenSpace Agility* approach into something rather different has been deeply satisfying. We think of OpenSpace Beta as the core method solving the seemingly impossible problem of how to transform entire organizations of any kind to Beta - and fast!

Through education and work, I have found opportunities to experience life in several countries and I got used to working in four languages - English, German, Spanish and Portuguese. These are also the languages that you might use to get in touch with me. E-mail: niels.pflaeging@redforty2.com. Find me on Twitter: @NielsPflaeging

Thank you!

We are thankful to Daniel Mezick for his inspiration, active support and encouragement, which helped make OpenSpace Beta happen in the first place. Our special thanks go to the authors of *The OpenSpace Agility Handbook* - Daniel Mezick, Deborah Pontes, Harold Shinsato, Louise Kold-Taylor and Mark Sheffield. For more about their work, visit *OpenSpaceAgility.com*

We are grateful to Harrison Owen, for making the introductory text on OpenSpace available for this handbook.

Thank you to our friend and graphic designer Ingeborg Scheer for the amazing OpenSpace Beta icon designs and illustrations, and for her great support with book & timeline design. Ingeborg's company & website: *dasign.de*

To illustrator Pia Steinmann, for the illustrations from the *Complexitools* book that are re-appearing in this volume.

To Deborah Hartmann Preuss, Francois Lavallée, Valentin Yonchev, Jeremy Brown and Matt Moersch, who reviewed & edited the manuscript and greatly improved the book.

To all our friends and peers who encouraged and supported us along the way, among them Kerstin Friedrich, Bill Pasmore, Paul Tolchinsky, Jon Husband, Harold Jarche, Francois Lavallée, Philippe Brière, Joe Krebs, Nils Oud, Doug Kirkpatrick, Jack Martin Leith, Bruce McTague, Michael Bungay Stanier, Frédéric Laloux, Chris Mahan, Jason Little, Stewart Desson, Kurt Nielsen, Mischa Ramseyer, Dennis Brunotte, Ben Heinl. A special thanks goes to Deborah Hartmann Preuss, for suggesting to Niels a few years back to get in touch with Daniel Mezick. "You have a lot in common", she said.

To Robin Fraser, co-founder of the Beyond Budgeting Round Table, who urged Niels, back in 2006, not to be afraid of inventing new words: "If we seriously mean to change the world," Robin said, "and make organizations far better places, then we must dare to create new terminology and language."

Get the OpenSpace Beta timeline poster and other useful products to support your Beta transformation. On OpenSpaceBeta.com

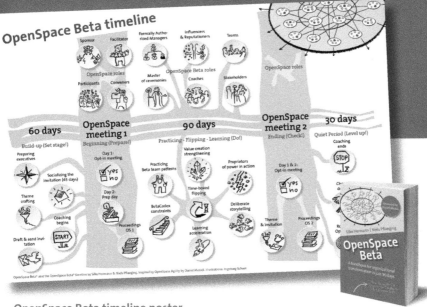

OpenSpace Beta timeline poster

A1 format.
Special color print for maximum impact.
International shipping.

OpenSpace Beta handbook

Book packages
with attractive discounts.
Free international shipping.

Ultimate Changemaker Box,
additional posters, card sets and more!

www.OpenSpaceBeta.com   www.RedForty2.com